Singapore
and Asia

Impact of the Global Financial Tsunami and Other Economic Issues

Editors

Sng Hui Ying
Chia Wai Mun

School of Humanities & Social Sciences,
Nanyang Technological University, Singapore

 **World Scientific**

NEW JERSEY · LONDON · SINGAPORE · BEIJING · SHANGHAI · HONG KONG · TAIPEI · CHENNAI

Published by

World Scientific Publishing Co. Pte. Ltd.

5 Toh Tuck Link, Singapore 596224

USA office: 27 Warren Street, Suite 401-402, Hackensack, NJ 07601

UK office: 57 Shelton Street, Covent Garden, London WC2H 9HE

Library of Congress Cataloging-in-Publication Data
NTU-MOE Seminars (2009 : Singapore)
   Singapore and Asia : impact of the global financial tsunami and other economic
issues / editors, Sng Hui Ying, Chia Wai Mun.
      p. cm.
   Includes bibliographical references and index.
   ISBN-13: 978-981-4280-45-7
   ISBN-10: 981-4280-45-3
1. Singapore--Economic policy--Congresses. 2. Asia--Economic policy--Congresses.
3. Financial crises--Singapore--Congresses. 4. Financial crises--Asia--Congresses.
5. Global Financial Crisis, 2008–2009. I. Sng, Hui Ying. II. Chia, Wai Mun. III. Title.
HC445.8.N78 2009
330.95957--dc22
                                           2009037583

British Library Cataloguing-in-Publication Data
A catalogue record for this book is available from the British Library.

Typeset by Stallion Press
Email: enquiries@stallionpress.com

Printed in Singapore.

Singapore
and Asia

Impact of the Global Financial Tsunami
and Other Economic Issues

Contents

Foreword

I have been very privileged to be associated with economic issues for most of my career in the public sector. I have come to realize the importance of careful and rigorous economic thinking as the basis of formulating sound public policy. Of course, economics is still more of an art than a science. Nevertheless a good understanding of its principles is still crucial as a necessary, if not sufficient, condition for sound and coherent economic policy.

It is therefore very interesting to note that NTU has organized annual seminars on topical economic issues with the Ministry of Education for teachers and students. This forum enables the transmission of economic knowledge acquired in academia to future generations of Singaporeans at large and its future leaders in particular. Given the imperative of sound economic policies for a small country immensely dependent on global trade, such a transfer of knowledge is vital for our future.

This book is a result of such a seminar. The contributors of the chapters have brought together materials that are highly topical like the current financial crisis and the global recession as well as analyses of the fundamentals of our economy.

Experts worldwide are debating whether this "tsunami" of the financial crisis could have been foreseen. A minority is of the view that this crisis is no "Black Swan" event and there were apparent signs of its impending arrival. Whatever the outcome of that debate, the more important issue is how economies like ours can withstand such periodic crises and emerge to take advantage of the opportunities thereafter.

Whilst the current financial crisis is gripping headlines every-day, as Singaporeans, we cannot forget the fundamentals that will govern our future prosperity and viability even as we prepare our-selves to weather this storm. I perceive the purpose and value of these NTU–MOE Seminars as a means to pass on the understand-ing of these economic fundamentals and realities. Given the sound economic foundations that we have built for ourselves so far, I believe that our economy does have the competitiveness and resilience to continue to prosper with the help of future genera-tions. On that note, I wish all the participants of the Seminar and the readers of the following chapters an interesting and thought-provoking journey.

March 2009   **Lam Chuan Leong**
Ambassador at Large, Ministry of Foreign Affairs
Chairman, Competition Commission of Singapore
Senior Fellow, Singapore Civil Service College
Adjunct Professor, Nanyang Technological University

Contributors

Abeysinghe, Tilak

Tilak Abeysinghe is Associate Professor of Economics at the National University of Singapore. He obtained his PhD in Economics/ Econometrics from the University of Manitoba and worked for the United States Agency for International Development (Colombo) before joining NUS in 1988. His research interests lie in both theoretical and applied econometric topics that include economics of ethnic peace and "selfish economic man". He has published in various reputable international journals like *Journal of Econometrics, Economics Letters, International Journal of Forecasting, Journal of Forecasting, Journal of Population Economics, Applied Economics, Review of International Economics* and *NBER* paper series. A major line of his research has been the econometric modeling of the Singapore economy, forecasting and policy analyses. As the coordinator of the Econometric Studies Unit since 1993, he has built a number of econometric models, one of which appears in the Routledge book, *The Singapore Economy: An Econometric Perspective*, that he co-authored with Choy Keen Meng. Policy analyses based on these models have appeared in news media frequently. Tilak has also held various important administrative responsibilities at NUS such as Deputy/Acting Head, Director of Economics Graduate Program, Deputy Director of the Singapore Center for Applied and Policy Economics and member of the Faculty Tenure and Promotion Committee.

Adireksombat, Kampon

Assistant Professor Kampon Adireksombat received his PhD from Michigan State University. His research interests include public finance, poverty, labor, demography and applied econometrics. Before joining NTU, he was a junior researcher at the Ministry of Finance in Thailand, an intern at the International Monetary Fund (IMF), and an instructor at Michigan State University. One of his research papers has been recently published in National Tax Journal. He is presently an Honorary Secretary of the Economic Society of Singapore and serves as an assistant editor to the Singapore Economic Review.

Chang Youngho

Chang Youngho is an Assistant Professor of Economics at the Division of Economics and the S. Rajaratnam School of International Studies (RSIS), Nanyang Technological University, Singapore. He is also an Adjunct Senior Fellow at the Energy Studies Institute (ESI), National University of Singapore. Apart from academic affiliations, he is a member of R&D Workgroup and Household Subcommittee for the National Climate Change Committee (N3C). Dr Chang specializes in the economics of climate change, the economics of renewable resources, energy and security, oil and economy, and electricity market deregulation. His current research interests are oil price fluctuations and macroeconomic performances, the economics of energy security, the transition of resource use in an economy, the economics of sustainability, energy use and climate change, and the effectiveness of a new market structure in a deregulated electricity market. He has published research papers in academic journals like *Econometric Theory, Economics Letters, Energy Policy, International Journal of Global Energy Issues*, and *International Journal of Electronic Business Management*. Dr Chang had worked as a landscape architect for two years in Korea and Saudi Arabia and a financial analyst for four years in Korea. He was a degree fellow at the East–West

Center, Hawaii and received his BSc (in Landscape Architecture) from the Seoul National University, MA (in Economics) from the Yonsei University and PhD (in Economics) from the University of Hawaii at Manoa, U.S.A.

Chew, Rosalind

Associate Professor Rosalind Chew teaches Labor Economics and Labor Relations in the Division of Economics at the Nanyang Technological University in Singapore. She received her graduate training in Economics both in Singapore (PhD, NUS) and Canada (MA and ABD, Western Ontario). She has four books to her credit, *Workers' Perceptions on Wage Determination in Singapore* (Times Academic Press), *The Singapore Worker: A Profile* (Oxford University Press), *Employment-Driven Industrial Relations Regimes* (Avebury) and *Wage Policies in Singapore: A Key to Competitiveness* (International Labor Organization). She has also published in various journals, including *Computational Economics, the International Journal of Manpower, Review of Pacific Basin Financial Markets and Policies*, and *Journal of Enterprising Communities*. She has received awards including Singapore National Book award and Honorary Professorship from Moscow External University of the Humanities. Her research interests include industrial relations, labor markets and entrepreneurship.

Chia Wai Mun

Chia Wai Mun obtained her Bachelor degree in Economics from the University of London with First Class Honors in 1996. She was then awarded the Datuk Paduka Hajjah Saleha Ali Outstanding Award for her exceptional academic performance at the international level in 1997. In 1998, with the support of the London School of Economics Scholarship, she pursued her Master's degree at the LSE. She obtained her PhD from Nanyang Technological University (NTU) in 2006. She is currently assistant professor at NTU. Before joining NTU, she was an industry analyst at the Federation of

Malaysian Manufacturers and a lecturer at HELP University College, Kuala Lumpur. Her current research interest focuses on international macroeconomics. She is an assistant editor to the *Singapore Economic Review*. She was also one of the research consultants to the ASEAN Secretariat working on managing net foreign assets in Singapore.

Choy Keen Meng

Choy Keen Meng obtained his PhD from NUS and his MSc from the London School of Economics and Political Science. Since his days as an economist at the Monetary Authority of Singapore from 1988 to 1992, he has been studying the Singapore economy. His publications are in the areas of business cycles, forecasting, and macroeconomics. He has acted as a consultant to the Department of Statistics, the Monetary Authority of Singapore, IE Singapore and the Vietnamese government. His chapter with Tilak Abeysinghe in this book is based on the large-scale macroeconometric model described in their book, *The Singapore Economy: An Econometric Perspective*. At Nanyang Technological University where he is assistant professor, he continues to issue economic prognostications on the Singapore economy.

Lam Chuan Leong

Mr Lam Chuan Leong is an Ambassador at Large with the Ministry of Foreign Affairs and the Chairman of the Competition Commission of Singapore. He also holds the appointments of Senior Fellow at the Singapore Civil Service College and an Adjunct Professor at the Nanyang Technological University. He is interested in the application of general management theories and macroeconomic management. His career has been involved in working on microeconomic issues in regard to economic regulation, monopolies and competition policy, pricing and market efficiency, privatization and transport economics.

Lim Chong Yah

Professor Lim Chong Yah was the founding Head of the Division
of Applied Economics, University of Malaya in Kuala Lumpur,
prior to becoming the Head of the Department of Economics and
Statistics (1977–1992) and the Dean of the Faculty of Arts and Social
Sciences (1971–1977) of the National University of Singapore. He
is currently the Albert Winsemius Chair Professor of Economics
and the Director of the Economic Growth Centre at the Nanyang
Technological University. Some of his long list of academic
publications have been translated into Chinese, Japanese and
Malay. One has gone into Braille. Professor Lim for 18 years was
the President of the Economic Society of Singapore and for 13 years
(1978–1991), the Editor of the *Singapore Economic Review*. For his
important contributions to scholarship and education, Soka
University of Japan conferred on him the "Doctor Honoris Causa"
in 1995, and three years later the Soka Gakkai International, Japan
awarded him with the "Chubu Award of Highest Glory". Hainan
University awarded him an Honorary Professorship and the
Hainan Provincial Government made him Honorary Chairman of
the Hainan University Council. Indiana University in the U.S. conferred on him the John W. Ryan Alumni Award for "Distinguished
Contributions to International Education". Professor Lim, however, is more than just a distinguished scholar, an eminent
educator and an internationally well-known academic development economist. For his important contributions to economic and
national development of Singapore and its trade union movement
as founding Chairman of the tripartite National Wages Council
(1972–2001) and founding Chairman of the Skills Development
Fund (SDF), the National Trade Unions Congress conferred on him
on Labor Day the Meritorious Service Award in 1985 and the
Distinguished Service Award in 1999. The Singapore Government
on Singapore's National Day awarded him with the Public Service
Star in 1996, the Meritorious Service Medal in 1983 and the
Distinguished Service Order in 2000. For his distinguished services
to the University and society, the National University of Singapore

in 2001 established a Lim Chong Yah Professorship at the Faculty of Arts and Social Sciences in his honor at the University.

Quah, Euston

Professor Euston Quah is Head of Economics and Acting Chair of School of Humanities and Social Sciences at the Nanyang Technological University. Prior to this, he was Vice-Dean, Faculty of Arts and Social Sciences at NUS; deputy director of the Public Policy Programme (now called the Lee Kuan Yew School of Public Policy); founding director of the Singapore Centre for Applied and Policy Economics (SCAPE); and Head of the Economics Department at NUS. He is a prolific writer with more than 40 peer-reviewed publications in international journals such as *Applied Economics*; *World Development*; *Environment and Planning*; *International Review of Law and Economics*; *Journal of Public Economic Theory*; *Journal of Environmental Management*; *American Journal of Economics and Sociology*; and some five books including *Cost-Benefit Analysis* (5th edition with E.J. Mishan published by Routledge, UK); *Siting Environmentally Unwanted Facilities* (with K.C. Tan published by Edward Elgar, UK) and *Economics and Home Production* (published by Ashgate, UK). He has a *Principles of Microeconomics* book with Gregory Mankiw (former Chairman of US Council of Economic Advisors and Harvard Professor). His work on measuring non-market goods has received good reviews in prestigious international journals such as *Economic Journal, Journal of Economic Literature*, and *Journal of Labour Economics*. Professor Quah has published some first Singapore studies relating to the environment such as the first cost of air pollution study of Singapore; the first study on the transboundary haze problem and its costs (published as an individual researcher); and the first study on the social cost of smoking in Singapore (published in the *Singapore Medical Journal*). He is an advisor to many government ministeries and had contributed to a number of key public projects. Professor Quah is editor of the *Singapore Economic Review*; co-editor of *International Gambling Studies* (edited at Australian National University); past associate editor of the *Asian Economic Journal* (edited at Chinese University of Hong Kong) and on the editorial board of the *ASEAN Economic Bulletin* (edited at ISEAS). He had served on the Board of Trustees of ISEAS; Council Member of SIIA; Adjunct Senior Research Fellow of IPS and is presently President of the Economic Society of Singapore.

Rana, Pradumna B.

Dr. Pradumna B. Rana is currently a senior research fellow at the Institute of South Asian Studies of the National University of Singapore. He was the senior director of the Asian Development Bank's (ADB's) Office of Regional Economic Integration which spearheaded the ADB's support for regional cooperation and integration in Asia. He joined the ADB in 1983 and held senior positions at the research and various operational departments. During 2007–2009 he was a senior fellow at the Nanyang Technological University of Singapore. Prior to joining the ADB, he was a Lecturer at the National University of Singapore and the Tribhuvan University (Nepal), a researcher at the Institute of Southeast Asian Studies in Singapore, and a consultant to the World Bank in Washington D.C. He obtained his PhD from Vanderbilt University where he was a Fulbright Scholar, and a Masters in Economics from Michigan State University and Tribhuvan University where he was a gold medalist. He has published widely in the areas of Asian economic development and integration, Asian financial crisis, business cycle co-movements, early warning systems of financial crisis, and policy reforms in transition economies. These include several books and articles in international scholarly journals including *Review of Economics and Statistics*, *Journal of International Economics*, *Journal of Development Economics*, *Journal of Asian Economics*, *World Development*, *Developing Economies*, and *Singapore Economic Review*. Recently, he co-authored a book on *South Asia: Rising to the Challenge of Globalization* (World Scientific) and co-edited a book on *Pan-Asian Integration: Linking East and South Asia* (Palgrave Macmillan). He is presently co-editing a book on *National Strategies for Regional Integration* (forthcoming 2009 Anthem Press, UK).

Sng Hui Ying

Sng Hui Ying is lecturer in Economics at the Nanyang Technological University (NTU). She obtained her PhD from NTU, and her MSocSci. and BSocSci. (Hons) from the National University of Singapore. She was awarded the *Lim Chong Yah Book Prize* for being the best candidate of the Master's degree programme. Her research areas include development economics, Southeast Asian economies and Singapore economy. Prior to joining NTU, she was a broadcast journalist/producer with Mediacorp News and a senior research officer with the Jurong Town Corporation. In 2002, she participated in a consultation project led by Professor Lim Chong Yah to advise the government of Mauritius on wage determination system and wage reform issues. She is the co-editor of the book *Singapore and Asia in a Globalized World: Contemporary Economic Issues and Policies* (World Scientific). Her research monograph, *Economic Growth and Transition: Econometric Analysis of Lim's S-Curve Hypothesis*, will be published in the 2nd half of 2009.

Sheffrin, Steven Mark

Steven M. Sheffrin is Professor of Economics at UC Davis. He joined the UC Davis faculty in 1976. He formerly served as both Department Chair of Economics and Dean of the Division of Social Sciences for 10 years. Sheffrin has been a visiting professor at Nuffield College (Oxford), the London School of Economics, Princeton University and Nanyang Technological University. He has also served as a financial economist with the Office of Tax Analysis and the U.S. Department of the Treasury and served as a member of the Board of Directors of the National Tax Association. Sheffrin also directs the Center for State and Local Taxation at UC Davis.

Sheffrin holds a BA from the College of Social Studies, Wesleyan University, and a PhD in economics from Massachusetts Institute of Technology. Sheffrin is the author of 10 books and monographs and over 100 articles in the fields of macroeconomics, public finance, and international economics. His most important books include *Rational Expectations* (2nd edition), *Property Taxes and Tax Revolts: The Legacy of Proposition 13*, both from Cambridge University Press, and *Economics: Principles, Applications, and Tools* (6th edition) from Prentice-Hall.

Tan Kong Yam

Tan Kong Yam is presently Director of the Asian Research Centre and Professor of Economics at the Nanyang Technological University in Singapore. Prior to joining NTU, he was a senior economist at the World Bank office in Beijing where he worked on issues of macro stabilization, integration of the fragmented domestic market, banking reform, international trade and investment as well as regional inequality. Prior to that, he was the chief economist of the Singapore government at the Ministry of Trade and Industry and Head of Department of Business Policy at the National University of Singapore (NUS).

He is a graduate of Princeton and Stanford Universities. His research interests are in international trade and finance, economic and business trends in the Asia Pacific region and economic reforms in China. He has published five books and numerous articles in major international journals including *American Economic Review, World Bank Economic Review, Long Range Planning, Australian Journal of Management*, etc. on economic and business issues in the Asia Pacific region. He served as board member at the Singapore Central Provident Fund Board (1984–96) and the National Productivity Board (1989–90). He has also consulted for many organizations including Temasek, GIC, Citigroup, IBM, ATT, BP, ABN-AMRO, Bank of China, People's Bank of China, EDB, Areva, Capitaland, Guangdong provincial government, Samsung,

Mauritius Government, Ministry of Trade and Industry, Mobil, Singapore Technology, etc.

Teo, Ernie

Assistant Professor Ernie Teo obtained his PhD from the University of New South Wales, Australia, where he also served as an associate lecturer. His teaching responsibilities at UNSW include Economic Strategy, Managerial Economics and Microeconomics. Ernie's main research interests are Industrial Organization, Game Theory and Applied Microeconomic Theory. His current research topics include Pricing of Multiplayer Online Games, Capital Budget Allocation (Colonel Blotto Games) and Strategic Economic Integration of Countries. He recently published in *The B.E. Journal of Theoretical Economics*.

PART I

ECONOMIC ANALYSIS OF THE GLOBAL FINANCIAL TSUNAMI

CHAPTER 1

The Deepening Global Recession and the Great Depression Fear*

LIM CHONG YAH

T he chapter gives four reasons why the world would not degenerate into a Great Depression as in the early 1930s, nor into a deepening slump. Time is on the side of the recovering process. The world-wide adopting of a cheap money and cheap credit policy and fiscal stimulus packages augers well for the road to recovery. The article also discusses the Ninja loans mortgage crisis and its spread to the whole US and world economy, and attempts by the Bush and Obama Administrations to contain the crisis. A brief comparison between crisis management in the US and China is also made. Finally, there is also a brief commentary on crisis management in Singapore.

---

* Lecture presented at the NTU–MOE Seminar 2009 at MOE on 16 March 2009 to Junior College teachers of economics in Singapore.

Road to Depression

The world will degenerate into a Great Depression if, among economic superpowers such as the US, China, Japan and the European Union:

(1) protectionism rears its ugly head,
(2) international trade war develops,
(3) competitive exchange rate devaluation unfolds, and
(4) pro-cyclical measures are pursued.

Fortunately, all nations on this earth, big or small, economic superpowers or otherwise, have eschewed (1), (2), (3) and (4). Historically, it was their blind pursuit of (1), (2), (3) and (4), especially among the then economic superpowers, that plunged the world into the Great Depression in the early 1930s. The contraction of governments was ubiquitous; all to save money to make ends meet. Mankind, including its governments, has since learned that the pursuit of (1), (2), (3) and (4) will plunge the sinking ship of recession into a more severe depression.

All governments in the early days of the 21st century pursue the following two macroeconomic anti-recession policies. One is to have a cheap money and cheap credit policy. And two is to have a sizeable budget stimulus or deficit financing. When the new US Secretary of State, Mrs Hillary Clinton, first made her maiden official visit to Beijing, she calmed the nerves of the Chinese by saying of the current global recession, "We are all not only in the same boat, but fortunately, we are all rowing in the same direction". Since the world is fighting the global recession at the same time, the probability of the world sliding into a Great Depression is almost zero, and that of a deepening recession into a global slump, very low indeed. Granted, there are others who may not hold this view.

Cheap Money Policy

Interest rate cuts

Effectiveness questionable

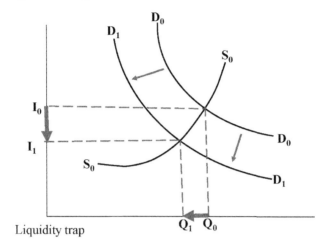

Liquidity trap

Figure 1.1:   The effects of a cheap credit policy.

Cheap Money Policy

Figure 1.1 shows the operation of a cheap money and cheap credit policy. Interest rate is reduced from I_0 to I_1, and notwithstanding that, the quantity of money in use is also reduced from Q_0 to Q_1, because the demand (liquidity preference) curve D_0 has fallen to D_1 consequent on the recession. Thus, even if the interest rate is reduced to near zero, it will have no impact on demand if the demand curve keeps falling, as symbolized by a constant shift of the curve moving south to the left.

Why must the demand curve shift southwards to the left, or decrease, in a recession? This is because, in a recession, the expected rate of return on capital declines. And it is this gloomy expectation that is associated with the concept of a liquidity trap, whereby the near zero interest rate may have no impact on the demand for money to satisfy the transaction motive. This was basically the situation faced by Japan in the 1990s after the property bubble burst in 1989. That decade was later called the "lost decade" for Japan.

Ninja Housing Loans

The current US recession has its genesis in the proliferation of NINJA loans almost throughout the USA. NINJA loans are loans given to borrowers by lending institutions, like Lehman Brothers, even though the borrowers have no income, no jobs and no assets. In other words, the lenders follow a high-consumption policy, lending very freely to every Tom, Dick or Harry. For a long time, this free lending policy posed no problem so long as the value of the housing assets kept rising. Even a second loan could be obtained, if the housing boom continued. No one would like to prick the housing bubble. The practice which brought much prosperity to the USA, however, was carried too far and for too long. The housing bubble finally burst. Once housing assets fell below the mortgaged loans, trouble on repayment surfaced. Foreclosures crept in. NINJA loans became toxic assets. NINJA loans were extended to car loans and consumer credit cards as well. Once the lenders were flush with so much toxic assets, the banking system became shaky. The falling values in the housing and banking sectors soon spread to other sectors as well, including the stock market and the automobile industry in a circular cumulative causation process. Because of international connectivity, the US credit crisis quickly spread to other parts of the world directly and indirectly in the first, second, and third round processes.

In other words, when asset prices kept rising, there was euphoria. Mr Alan Greenspan, who was then the much-acclaimed Chairman of the US Federal Reserve Bank basked in much of the euphoric limelight not just in the US and but also in the world. When asset prices fell, there was the crisis. The crisis gained momentum in the last remaining years of the Bush Administration. Neither Mr Bush nor his two most important financial and economic ministers, namely, Professor Ben Bernanke and Mr Henry Paulson, could stop the decline. Professor Bernanke is the Chairman of the US Federal Reserve and Mr Paulson was the US Treasury Secretary.

Early Attempts at Fighting the Crisis

The epicentre of the global crisis is in Wall Street in the USA. In the early period of the US crisis, Professor Ben Bernanke, as the Fed Chairman, took centre stage with Treasury Secretary Henry Paulson remaining relatively silent; and President George Bush even more reticent. Monetarism, not fiscal stimulus, was to provide the answer, the cure. More than that, the diagnosis of the crisis was equivocal. Bernanke expressed the fear of inflation instead of recession or deflation. Thus, the interest rate cut was very piecemeal, and consequently, very frequent. This vicissitude and equivocation in the diagnosis and prescription must have contributed to the spread, breath and depth of the crisis. There was no attempt to nip the crisis in the bud through clear and resolute monetary and fiscal measures.

When the crisis deepened, Henry Paulson finally stepped in. That was considered too late, and many, including the 2008 Economics Nobel Prize Winner Professor Paul Krugman, would add, too little had been done. When Paulson asked Congress to approve the release of funds for fiscal stimulus, he changed his mind on the use of the money. He said that it was to be used to bailout toxic debts, not for infrastructural development and rejuvenation. Then he left office when President Obama succeeded President Bush as the 44th President of the USA.

Figure 1.2 shows the role of fiscal response to bring back falling income and falling investment resulting from a deepening recession. Private sector demand D_0, in a recession, falls to D_1. The objective of public policy is how to bring demand back from D_1 to D_0. Since monetary policy in itself cannot lift private sector demand back to D_0, fiscal policy is resorted to. In other words, public sector demand is brought in to counterbalance the falling private sector demand.

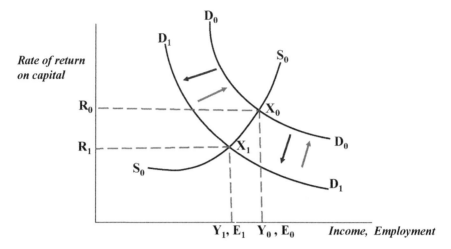

Figure 1.2: Theory on fiscal response (A simplified model).

Two important aspects of the fiscal stimulus must be considered here. They have often been overlooked in public discussion. One is the composition of the stimulus expenditure. Two is the financing of the fiscal stimulus. The composition may, very roughly, be broken down into two parts: one, income transfer in favor of direct consumption; and two, the building up of income-bearing assets which will lead to increase in consumption in the second round. The second approach implies that there are such projects that merit fiscal support and not all such projects are readily available or can be made available within short notice. The US appears to be short of supply in such strategic projects. Strategy one can aggravate the already bad balance of payments deficit on current account in the US with little or no impact on productivity and competitiveness, particularly external competitiveness.

The financing of the fiscal stimulus, too, has often been sidelined. If the country is well prepared for such an economic aberration, it will finance it from the strategic accumulated foreign exchange reserves such as in the case of China and Singapore. If it is not pre-prepared, such as in the case of the United States, it may have to be financed from foreign borrowing and fiduciary issue, which is a euphemism for printing of more money. Fiduciary issues can be inflationary. A small amount, in the US and US only, however, might help the economy to break away from the liquidity trap. A surfeit can easily lead to inflationary pressures and exchange rate devaluation. If the rest of the world would continue to accumulate US dollars as an international reserve currency, fear of exchange rate devaluation need not happen in the case of the US. External borrowing will only increase the already high external indebtedness of the US, accumulated under the Bush Administration under its budget deficit program during the NINJA loans boom years.

The "Change" Strategy

When President Obama won the election on 4th November 2008, there was great expectation of his ability to handle the deepening recession. His first-rate rhetoric had convinced everyone both within and outside the US. He meant business by focusing his whole attention in transforming the recession into recovery. The cheap money policy was followed with more vigor together with a very much bigger budget stimulus.

Unfortunately, there was many a slip between the cup and the lips. President Obama needed a good and credible and able economic team to manage the *modus operandi* in the recovery program. He appointed two previous Bush Administration's luminaries to manage his urgent economic affairs. They are Mr Timothy Geithner as Treasury Secretary and Professor Ben Bernanke who would continue as the Fed Chairman. Dr Larry Summers, a former Treasury Secretary, is to be his chief economic adviser. All three are considered to be closely connected with Wall Street. All three have different degrees of association with the previous free-spending and free-wheeling policy of achieving affluence through high consumption.

Mr Timothy Geithner, the head of the trio, was immediately handicapped by President Obama's inability to have the two much-needed deputies for him. Besides, Mr Geithner nearly opened up a possible trade war with China by accusing China of contributing to the US balance of payment problem. He too incurred the wrath of Europeans and others by having an "only buy American" and "use American labor only" policies. To them, that was protectionism's ugly head. He has other incipient problems. Fortunately, other more-reasoned members of the Obama Administration, including Vice President Joe Biden, Secretary of State Mrs Hillary Clinton, Economic Advisor Dr Larry Summers and the President himself stepped in to sideline the issues so that the Administration could concentrate on more urgent domestic recovery matters through appropriate fiscal stimulation, including arresting the widening toxic debt problem and the very important declining automobile industry. Foreign economic issues should not be a red herring for the task of getting out of the US domestic economic crisis under the overall "change" policy of the new Administration. It is a pity that cost-cutting measures seem to be politically inappropriate.

However, both the toxic debt problem, increasing in spread and depth with time, and the Achilles' heel in the three US automobile icons, defy an easy solution. Again, the Obama Administration appears indecisive and equivocal in strategy: the wavering between the "to be or not to be" in following the lender of last resort function and the time-honored and time-cherished American philosophy of pursuing a policy of creative destruction, even for important corporations and industries such as these. The new Administration's unexpected vicissitude and equivocation, reminiscent somewhat of the Bush Administration, has contributed to prolonging the crisis in the USA and, therefore, the world. But the three Wise Men in the USA, the three economic tzars, one should not forget, are basically also rowing in the same direction as the rest of the world in advocating a big fiscal stimulus and a cheap credit policy. The world is in the same team.

Comparison with China

China, in PPP terms, has become nearly half the size of the USA. She can use "moral suasion" as an instrument of monetary policy.

US, however, appears to be handicapped in this. "Moral suasion" means the central bank can persuade the commercial banks, most of whom are state-owned banks in China, to lend out more money to customers. On fiscal stimulus, China has at least two comparative advantages. One is that she has the largest foreign reserves in the world, nearly US$2 trillion. Two is that she has a good supply of worthwhile projects to implement. China has a rolling five-year development plan. She can thus bring forward the projects to serve as an anti-recession move as well. Under the circumstances, should one be surprised when Chinese Prime Minister Wen Jiabao announced that China in 2009 would be able to have a positive GDP growth rate of eight percent? By way of contrast, USA would probably have a reported negative rate of three to four percent like that of many other developed economies. So, fiscal stimulus may work differently in different countries. India and Vietnam too have reported a positive growth rate of between five and six percent for 2009. Of note is that China, India and Vietnam are developing countries with more potential for infrastructural development than developed countries, like the US or Japan and Western Europe.

The Singapore Scenario

As this lecture is given in Singapore and to Singapore's teachers of economics, I would like to make a few observations on the domestic economic scene. The global recessionary impact on Singapore is very great, particularly on GDP and export income, but not on the unemployment rate. This is because of the flexible wage policy pursued in Singapore, resorting to retrenchment only as a last resort.

Besides, the government has introduced two important new measures to combat the recession. One is called the Job Credit Scheme under which an employer will be refunded 12 percent of an employee's wages for a period of three months, for employees paid less than $2,500 per month. This provides an incentive for employers not to retrench workers, particularly lowly-paid workers.

Two is that, under the Special Risk Sharing Initiative (SRI), the government is prepared to guarantee up to 80 percent of the bank loans for a period of one year should there be any default. This is to encourage banks to lend to SME borrowers and to prevent the liquidity trap scenario from developing in Singapore. To finance these two temporary measures, the government obtained a portion of the fund, a very small portion indeed, from its huge accumulated reserves. This withdrawal is being made for the first time in Singapore's history as the severity of the fall in export income and GDP are the most severe in Singapore's history since the Great Depression.

Notwithstanding such innovative anti-recessionary measures, and the strong economic fundamentals in Singapore, the official forecast is that Singapore is likely to have a serious negative growth rate in 2009. The validity of this negative forecast is based primarily on a pessimistic forecast of the world economy. It may also be partly due to the fact that in making the forecast, more emphasis is given to year-on-year *(y-o-y)*, quarter-to-quarter comparison of GDP and export figures instead of, in the recovery phase, the more relevant quarter-on-quarter *(q-o-q)* and month-on-month *(m-o-m)* comparison in the same year and not over the previous year (2008), when there was a boom in the first two quarters (Q1 08 and Q2 08). There was also a tendency in Singapore, in a deepening recession, to excessively publicize only retrenchment figures but not within the context of total job creation for the periods in question.

Global Silver Linings

As stated earlier, unlike during the Great Depression, man has learned how to combat global recessions. All governments, big and small, have adopted cheap money and cheap credit policy and all have a fiscal stimulus package or packages. If we *sigma* these fiscal packages, the total (the sum-of-parts) can be a staggering figure. There might be an infrastructural boom, if not some threats of over-heating in this sector with time. The credit and banking sector, too, may get an early stimulation. Already, stock markets all over the world have reacted positively to this joint global stimulus, the day-to-day volatile mood and poor company reports, based on past performances, notwithstanding. The stock markets are often used as fairly dependable leading indicators in macroeconomic forecasting.

My own conclusion is that there has been in more recent months a deceleration in the negative growth rates in many economies in the world, including the US, and this deceleration will continue until probably the last two quarters of 2009 when more positive growth rates would appear. Time is in favor of recovery, including in the USA, and Singapore will be positively affected by this global upturn.

References

Lim, C. Y. (2009). The Asian Financial Crisis. In *Southeast Asia: The Long Road Ahead* (3rd Ed.), Chap. 12. Singapore: World Scientific.

Lim, C. Y. (2009). The Asian Financial Crisis and the Sub-Prime Mortgage Crisis: A Dissenting View. In Chia Wai Mun and Sng Hui Ying (eds.), *Singapore and Asia in a Globalized World: Contemporary Economic Issues and Policies*, pp. 105–120. Singapore: World Scientific.

Lim, C. Y. (2008). The US Financial Crisis, the Moral Hazard Problem and the Two US Administrations. Special Lecture presented at The Philip Kotler Center for ASEAN Marketing — Jakarta CMO Club, Indonesia.

Lim, C. Y. (2007). The International Monetary Fund and Exchange Rate Crisis Management. *Singapore Economic Review*, 52(3). Special Issue on the Exchange Rate Systems and Policies in Asia, pp. 285–294.

Lim, C. Y. (2003). Macroeconomic Management: Is Keynesianism Dead? *Singapore Economic Review*, 48(1), pp. 1–12.

CHAPTER 2

The Surprising Resurgence
of Fiscal Policy

STEVEN MARK SHEFFRIN

As recently as in 2003, Alan Auerbach of UC Berkeley wrote that his research strongly suggested "continued caution in the use of discretionary fiscal policy" and greater focus on the use of automatic stabilizers. Merely seven years later, the United States, Europe, and China enacted massive increases in government spending and taxes, with the US package leading the group at $800 billion, over five percent of GDP. Large numbers of European countries are now projected to exceed their self-imposed fiscal limits, and China is planning massive infrastructure investment in a wide variety of sectors. While the financial crisis of 2008 was unusually severe, how did we make this transition from cautious use to fiscal cannons?

This paper suggests that, for over 30 years, there has been a disjunction between the views of policymakers and politicians on the use of discretionary fiscal policy and the views of most academic economists. During this period, macroeconomists devoted much of their energies to exploring the theoretical foundations of macroeconomics, explicitly rejecting the neo-classical synthesis that propelled macroeconomic stabilization policy through the 1960s.

This shift in viewpoint was largely, but not limited to, the focus on expectations, intertemporal issues, and equilibrium models of the business cycles. Politicians, while more certainly more prone to tax cuts, had not totally abandoned fiscal policy as a stabilization tool. As a result of this disjunction, academic economists were not in a strong position to convey detailed technical advice on the structure of the proposed stimulus packages in 2009. Politicians were largely left to their own resources. As Alan Auerbach commented at the American Economic Association annual meeting in January 2009, "We have spent so many years thinking that discretionary fiscal policy was a bad idea, that we have not figured out the right things to do to cure a recession that is scaring all of us".[1]

Several forces still operated in academia in favor of discretionary fiscal policy. First, there was the lost decade in Japan, initially caused by over-speculation in equity and real estate markets. The economic and policy environment of mild deflation with zero interest rates and erratic fiscal policy had attracted the interest of a number of economists, including the influential voices of Ben Bernanke and Paul Krugman. Second, there were a few voices in the intellectual academic wilderness. Alan Blinder, amazingly prescient in 2004, wrote, "So my overall conclusion runs something like this. Under *normal* circumstances, monetary policy is a far better candidate for stabilization policy than fiscal policy... That said, however, there will be occasional *abnormal* circumstances in which monetary policy can use a little help, or maybe a lot, in stimulating the economy". (Italics in the original) He goes on to list as abnormal circumstances, long and severe recessions, nominal interest rates close to zero, and sudden decreases in aggregate demand. He surely would add the 2008 financial crisis to this list. But even Blinder had to preface his defense of fiscal policy with a disclaimer of its effects in normal times and to remark that, "It is perfectly appropriate for there to be 10–20 conferences on monetary policy for every one in fiscal policy".

---

[1] Louis Uchitelle (2009).

The discussion of current fiscal policy has been primarily focused on using changes in spending and taxation to increase aggregate demand. Another traditional image of fiscal policy has been "pump-priming", that is taking actions to recharge the private sectors' own spending and then disappear into the background. Pump-priming can be justified by macroeconomic models with multiple equilibria, which may have some applicability in the current environment.

From Enthusiasm to Skepticism: A Capsule Intellectual History

The high watermark for postwar fiscal policy most likely coincided with the publication of Alan Blinder's and Robert Solow's essay, "Analytical Foundations of Fiscal Policy", in a 1974 Brookings volume. The paper summarized the state of the art in implementing fiscal policy, including separating discretionary policy from automatic stabilizers, calculation of multipliers for alternative policy instruments, and discussions of the consequences of lags. There was also an emphasis, quite peculiar in retrospective, on the long-run consequences of bond versus money financing of deficits. Long run was defined as budget balance including interest payments on bonds. If an increase in the supply of bonds had a net increase on aggregate demand — the wealth effects in consumption exceeding any increase in money demand — then bond-financed government spending was necessarily more expansionary in the long run. This result arose because interest payments on a now larger stock of bonds would need to be financed through additional tax revenues. Higher tax revenues could occur through an expansion of output (in an pure Keynesian world) or an increase in tax revenues through prices in a setting of non-indexed taxes. Although this work continued to attract academic interest for a few years, it quickly became overtaken with major intellectual currents that were sweeping macroeconomics.

The first current was the "natural rate" revolution engineered by Milton Friedman and Edmund Phelps, now both Nobel laureates.

Their contributions undercut the foundations of the traditional aggregate supply models that were used in Keynesian models and that had been an integral component of the multiplier effect from fiscal policy. While expectations were incorporated into macroeconomic models early in the 1970s in the form of a modified aggregate supply curve, increasing attention now began to be paid both to expectations and the transition from the short to long run.

The second current was the rational expectations revolution led by Robert E. Lucas, Jr. and Thomas J. Sargent. As recounted in Sheffrin (1996), expectations of economic agents were the key drivers in this intellectual movement as embodied in the famous "Lucas critique". Macroeconomic models embodied decision rules of agents made in stochastic environments that included endogenous government policy. Understanding economic behavior in that setting required understanding how agents would respond to changes in policy rules as well as to true one-time shocks. Even defining discretionary policy in that setting became problematic: when is an action a change in a policy rule or when is it a "shock"? If it were the former, then a completely new type of econometric model was needed for analysis. If the latter, how could a deliberate policy choice, made in a particular economic environment, truly be classified as a one-time shock?

In formulating their expectations, it was required that agents look into the future. Incorporating the expectations of sophisticated agents into even standard Keynesian models could produce unexpected results. For example, an anticipated contractionary policy — such as a future decrease in government purchases — would actually be expansionary. As Blanchard (1981) recounted, the future decrease in government spending would eventually lower interest rates. However, the anticipated decrease in interest rates would lower interest rates immediately stimulating investment spending. Thus, private spending rises before public spending falls and the economy expands. Empirical evidence was later put forth for related propositions by Giavazzi and Pagano (1990).

In principle, this has radical implications for fiscal policy — flipping it on its head. If credible long run decreases in spending required some commitment to even mild decreases now, then even current spending cuts could be expansionary. As we will recount, this line of reasoning had later political impact.

A second intertemporal focus was on understanding the impact of budget deficits. Robert Barro (1974) brought back "Ricardian equivalence" to the economics profession. With an intertemporal budget for the government — either enforced through infinitely-lived agents or through generational dynasties — given a path of government spending, taxes could only be postponed. The upshot was any level of government spending imposed the same burden. All deficit financing could do was to change the timing of the tax payments — not the present value of current and future tax obligations.

Economists long-recognized from Milton Friedman's work on permanent income that a temporary tax cut would have less effect on private consumption than a permanent tax cut. In Barro's world, all tax cuts were temporary and had no effect whatsoever on spending. While economists had a field day exploring the theoretical ramifications and empirical viability of Ricardian equivalence, the renewed emphasis on deficits coincided with political concerns that were to emerge.

One of the intellectual descendants of the joint natural rate and rational expectations revolutions was the birth of Real Business Cycle Theory. If the economy only deviated from full employment because of expectational failure and expectational mistakes were limited because of rationality, then something else was needed to drive the ups and downs of the business cycle. Edward Prescott, also a Nobel laureate, proposed doing away with expectational shocks and, instead relied on shocks to technology to drive the business cycle. An important part of this research program was how shocks to relative prices — whether through technology or taxes or spending policies — drove economic fluctuations. Taxes and spending mattered now, but not in a Keynesian demand side framework, but through the supply side of the economy. Fiscal policy was properly a branch of applied public finance. Changes in government spending may have "income effects" as in microeconomic theory and certainly tax rates change incentives through their effects on marginal rates of return. Again, political entrepreneurs with their own agenda and stories also focused on the supply side.

Thus, by the early 1980s the entire foundation of conventional fiscal policy had collapsed. Propositions such as the following were certainly discussed actively among the brightest economists in the country:

(1) The way to stimulate the economy is to promise to cut govern-
    ment spending and perhaps even cut government spending
    immediately.
(2) Tax cuts — apart from changing incentives and relative prices —
    have no effects whatsoever on aggregate demand and spending.
(3) The focus of fiscal policy should be on the marginal incentives
    from taxation, not the traditional multiplier effects.

If these accounts were taken seriously, traditional fiscal policy — as envisaged by Blinder and Solow — was clearly dead.

There were other strands of research that served to undercut the foundations of discretionary fiscal policy. In one strand, it was the politicians who took the lead in recognizing the strategic role of tax cuts and deficit financing in their ideological battles. As early as 1981, Donald Regan, Secretary of Treasury under President Ronald Reagan, remarked to the US Treasury taxation staff that he was in favor of indexing the income tax (which did occur several years later) because the additional revenue that non-indexing would bring into the Treasury was "putting sand in Congress's sandbox". In a slightly different vein, Newt Gingrich, former Republican Speaker of the House of Representatives, remarked that he was "tired of Republicans being tax collectors for the welfare state". Both Regan and Gingrich were referring to the political role that tax cuts or increases could play in the battle for the size of government. Regan's view, later known as "starve the beast", implicitly assumed that the level of taxation deter-mined the level of spending. Gingrich, on the other hand, seemed to imply that Republicans had adopted a policy of fiscal responsibility in which spending plans by Democrats led to later tax increases.

Hoover and Sheffrin (1992) and much later Romer and Romer (2007a) explored the alternative causal mechanisms underlying these two views. Hoover and Sheffrin did find evidence that taxes caused spending prior to mid-1960s but later there appeared to be mutual interdependence. Romer and Romer did not find government spending to increase subsequent to the historical episodes they characterized as "discretionary".

Alesina and Tabellini (1990) explored the strategic role that deficit financing per se could play in ideological battles over the size of government. A party that wanted to limit government but feared the alternative party that wished to expand government would succeed could run large budget deficits. These deficits would constrain the large government party from their preferred expansion. Perhaps the Clinton administration witnessed this in reverse, as it left a large budget surplus to President George W. Bush who subsequently used it to facilitate an expansion of his own favorite programs and substantial tax cuts.

Another strand of research that highlighted the limitations of tax cuts in discretionary fiscal policy followed in the footsteps of Milton Friedman's work on permanent income and the limited impact of temporary tax cuts. In theory, if households were liquidity constrained then even temporary tax cuts could lead to additional consumption spending as this allowed households to smooth their consumption pattern over time. Even recent evidence on this question is mixed. Slemrod and Shapiro (2003) surveyed households who claimed that they would save most of the 2001 rebates, designed to be permanent first installments on a tax cut. However, Elmendorf and Furman (2008) discussed evidence from studies of the same episode that show lower income and households that are more likely to be liquidity constrained spent a high fraction of that rebate. The continuing controversies, however, did raise questions about the efficacy of tax cuts in stimulating the economy.

What Were the Politicians Up To?

The history of postwar fiscal policy in the United States has taken many twists and turns and a full survey would require a complete monograph. Useful overviews on fiscal policy are provided in O'Sullivan, Sheffrin, and Perez (2009) and Romer and Romer (2007b). Beginning in the early 1960s, we can identify four distinct periods in postwar US fiscal policy: aggressive Keynesian polices followed by a decade of inaction, policies rationalized by supply side concerns, preoccupations with deficits, and an extemporaneous approach to policy formation.

The most aggressive use of fiscal policy occurred during the administration of President Johnson and known as the Kennedy tax cuts, as they were enacted after John F. Kennedy's assassination. Walter Heller, the Chairman of the Council of Economic Advisers, aggressively pushed Keynesian policies but also advocated for lower marginal tax rates as well. The economy grew rapidly after the tax cuts, although the source of fiscal stimulus was due to the buildup for the war in Vietnam. The fiscal stimulus, coupled with monetary accommodation, led to increases in inflation. A tax surcharge, enacted in 1968, was designed to slow down the growth in aggregate demand but its temporary nature limited its efficacy.

The 1970s saw little in discretionary fiscal policy. There were periodic tax cuts, but these were largely to offset the tax revenues that were accruing through a combination of progressivity and lack of indexation. Policymakers were clearly preoccupied with inflation and the unfortunate oil shocks that created stagflationary dilemmas.

The 1970s, however, did witness the birth of supply side economics. Although some of the political rhetoric, as exemplified by the Laffer curve's inverse relation of tax revenues and tax rates was simplistic, the basic idea of lowering the burden of government goes back at least to ancient China. Yu Juo, one of the 12 wise men who succeeded Confucius, was confronted by skeptical bureaucrats who did not believe in his advice to cut tax rates from 30 to 10 percent during a famine. His response was vintage Laffer: "Cutting taxes and limiting your expenses allow people to raise their standard of living. Afterwards, you will no longer need to worry about famine and shortage".[2] As we noted earlier, these sentiments were in line with the birth of real business cycle models and their emphasis on relative prices.

The administration of Ronald Reagan embraced supply side principles in its major tax act of 1981. The emphasis was on the reduction of marginal tax rate reductions for individuals and accelerated depreciation and tax credits for business. Although the rhetoric was clearly supply side-oriented, the same tax cuts also had large income effects and increased consumers' disposable incomes. These "Keynesian" effects were indeed welcomed as offsets to the aggressive disinflation engineered by Federal Reserve Chairman Paul Volcker and implicitly endorsed by the Reagan Administration. In one sense, these tax cuts were effectively the first major Keynesian stimulus package enacted in 20 years.

The combination of tax cuts, a deep recession, and a military buildup to challenge the Soviet Union all combined to create large budget deficits. These deficits began to dominate fiscal policy discussions. A series of balance-budget amendments circulated through the Congress and nearly became enacted into law. Instead, various "doomsday" budget devices — the most famous being Gramm–Hollings — attempted to tie Congress's hand. By the early 1990s, they even made President George H.W. Bush renege on his ill-fated declaration, "read my lips, no new taxes" much to his political detriment. Ironically, Fed Chairman Alan Greenspan's tight monetary policy led to a mild recession, ending President Bush's hopes for re-election. A mild fiscal stimulus may have offset the

---

[2] Confucius Biography at http://www.ct.taipei.gov.tw/EN/01-history/hst2.html.

tight money policy, which the Bush administration had lobbied against unsuccessfully.

The deficit preoccupations continued into the Clinton administration. President Bill Clinton had wanted to enact a stimulus package after he took office. His advisers, including former Goldman–Sachs adviser Robert Rubin, preached a mantra of reducing deficits would prove expansionary — similar to the academic ideas advanced by Blanchard a decade earlier. Rubin predicted the bond market would respond favorably to deficit reduction through lower interest rates which, in turn, would stimulate the economy. James Carville, a skeptical Clinton political adviser, remarked: "I used to think if there was reincarnation, I wanted to come back as the President or the Pope or a .400 baseball hitter, but now I want to come back as the bond market. You can intimidate everybody".[3] Clinton raised the top marginal tax rates, which were left in place during his two-terms.

The Democrats lost the Congress to the Republicans after President Clinton's first two years in office. The Clinton administration had little appetite for tax cuts and the Republican Congress had little appetite for increased social spending. This stalemate, coupled with higher income tax rates and a surge in tax revenues from capital gains taxation during the high-tech boom, led to an unprecedented budget surplus.

President George Bush entered office with this surplus. It was so unprecedented that alarm bells went off in some quarters, with fears that continuing surpluses would retire all the government debt held by the public, thereby making it impossible for the Fed to conduct open-market policies. Within the Bush administration, the focus was on the opportunity to roll back the Clinton tax cut and provide additional tax relief to lower-income individuals and businesses as well. There were many different rationales for this tax cut — a slowing economy following the collapse of the tech boom which justified Keynesian style rhetoric, supply side

---

[3] Citation: http://www.global-investor.com/quote/3497/James-Carville.

rationales for the personal marginal rate cuts and business incentives, money in the pocket through initial rebates that were a component of the ongoing tax reduction, and social engineering through increased child-care credits. Although President Bush would later be characterized as rigid and ideological in his approach to foreign policy, on domestic policy he was foremost a pragmatist. With this and later policies, Bush decided what he would like to see and the rhetoric justifying these actions was left to his aides or speechwriters.

The events of September 11th and the ensuing downturn gave another opportunity for tax policy. In 2003, another tax bill was enacted, which had many diverse features, including moving up previously scheduled rate cuts, increased tax credits for children, and a change long sought-after by the business community, a reduction of taxes on dividends and capital gains. This smorgasbord of tax changes made it impossible for future politicians to totally abandon the Bush programs. During his campaign, Barack Obama was careful to state that he wished to repeal the Bush tax cuts only for high-income individuals and even limited increases in dividends and capital gains taxes.

A shift in the mood about discretionary policy was clearly evident in early 2008 when a broad political coalition emerged around tax rebates. A sagging economy, a weakened President Bush from the battles of the Iraq war, a resurgent Democratic Congress all converged on a tax rebate scheme that was enacted rather quickly and cleanly. An intellectual coalition supported a rebate that was "timely, temporary, and targeted". Timely, to have immediate impact; temporary, to avoid worsening long run deficits; and targeted at lower-income individuals who had higher marginal propensities to consume, rather than save the tax cut. The coalition included economists from the Brooking Institution's Hamilton project, receiving sage advice from Robert Rubin; Lawrence Summers, former Harvard President and Treasury Secretary and soon to be President Obama's chief economic adviser; and even Martin Feldstein, a moderate Republican and president of the National Bureau of Economic Research. Later, after the rebates were enacted, Feldstein believed they were ineffective and opposed similar policies.[4]

Of course, the financial crisis did not end in mid-2008, nor did the thirst for even larger stimulus packages recede. Indeed, the coalition in favor of grander packages featuring more spending increased in size. President Bush's weakness and eclecticism may have allowed fiscal policy some room to maneuver by 2008, but another major historical episode echoed in policy debates in late 2008.

The Key Role of the Japanese Experience

Fiscal policy in 2008 and 2009 was formulated with the experiences of the Japanese economy during the 1990s in mind. But what were those experiences? Observers really only agreed on two things. First, Japan was mired in a decade-long recession brought on originally by over-speculation. Second, nominal interest rates were pushed close to zero with little effect, a scenario that brought the term "liquidity trap" back into vogue.

Policy observers were in less agreement about the stabilization policies that were employed. With regard to monetary policy, the classic analysis of how to escape from a liquidity trap, for example in Krugman (1998), is to commit to an inflation that would lower the expected real rate of interest. This would call for a massive increase in the monetary base and certainly was not the policy that the Japanese government utilized during that period, which as Kuttner and Posen (2001) discussed, was rather conventional. However, with the collapse of the banking system and "zombie banks", some questioned whether any monetary policy — even creative ones — would have immediate impacts. The perception, however, is that monetary policy was not an effective instrument for the Japanese during their long period of economic malaise.

---

[4] Martin Feldstein (2009) believed that there were generally too few policies that affected economic incentives.

What about fiscal policy? Here opinions also differ. On one hand, nearly everyone agrees that a substantial portion of the increased public works spending in the 1990s had dubious public value and analogies abound to Keynes' pyramids.[5] Yet, in standard models of aggregate demand, the social value of expenditures is not the key issue. In assessing fiscal policies, what matters are the net contributions to aggregate demand through changes in government spending and taxes and transfer payments that can be considered autonomous.

Disentangling the contributions of discretionary fiscal policy requires an effort to separate policy changes from endogenous movements of both taxation and spending. This is particularly relevant for taxation, as tax revenues clearly depend on the state of the economy. Kuttner and Posen (2001) used a structural vector-autoregressive model (with three variables: expenditure, taxes, and GDP) to try to untangle some of these issues. They found that the tax and spending multipliers from "shocks" to each have the conventional signs, although the tax multipliers were larger than the government spending multipliers. They also found little evidence for Ricardian effects that some had conjectured for Japan, with its emphasis on family and intergenerational connections, as well as its longer-run structural deficit problems.

Then why did fiscal policy fail to work in Japan? To echo E. Cary Brown's remarks on the 1930s: because it was not tried. Deficits did expand in the 1990s, but largely because tax revenues were flat in a slumping economy. Concerned with long run deficits stemming from an aging society, the government was reluctant to dramatically increase deficits. With respect to tax policy, the government first adopted a mild expansionary policy that was explicitly labeled as temporary, then reversed it with an *increase* in the value-added tax in 1997. This contractionary action was well-known in the economic community. It later adopted a more expansionary policy but not terribly aggressively. Government spending increases were often followed by subsequent tax

---

[5] Especially, Japanese economists. See Eackler (2009).

increases, thereby offsetting some of the stimulus. Indeed, Kuttner and Posen find that fiscal "shocks" derived from their structural vector-autoregressions indicate that fiscal policy was generally contractionary.

While the Japanese experience was not uncontroversial, it did plant the seeds of several ideas that later became important in the stabilization discussions of 2008 and 2009. First, with a troubled financial system and very low interest rates, conventional monetary policy would not deliver the goods. The Federal Reserve under Ben Bernanke clearly absorbed this lesson embarking on a period of remarkable experimentation and improvisation. Second, fiscal policy was still an important tool — but it had to be used aggressively and consistently, unlike the way it was used in Japan. And, finally, government spending could still be expansionary, but public inefficiencies could easily accompany fiscal expansions.

Pump-Priming: An Alternative Model of Fiscal Policy

Traditional discussions of discretionary fiscal policy, despite their differences, have one thing in common. They envision changes in taxation and spending as shifting the aggregate demand curve. Debates typically are on whether the proposed changes in taxation and spending actually shift the aggregate demand curve or whether they are short-circuited, for example, by taxpayers saving rebates or government spending directly crowding out private spending.

The difficulty with the conventional view for a severe recession, however, is that if changes in spending or taxation are only meant to be temporary, then the shift in aggregate demand will have to be reversed. Reversing aggregate demand will cause a deflationary shock and thus would have to be precisely timed to avoid this problem. Our knowledge of the lags in economic policy and the dynamics of private spending are sufficiently murky that such a reversal could cause major difficulties. These would be particularly pronounced for the major stimulus packages that were debated in 2008 and 2009.

There is an alternative view of the role of fiscal policy, associated with the rather dated term of "pump-priming". The idea is that you need to move the lever of the pump up and down a few times to "prime the pump" but later the normal pumping action brings up the water from the well. Fiscal policy based on the idea of pump-priming would suggest that taking some significant but temporary actions would then allow the economy to resume its normal fashion. In this setting, there would not be a "fiscal reversal" problem.

A natural way to model this view of fiscal policy is to use a simple macroeconomic model that features multiple equilibria. Such models were originally developed in the literature of coordination failure (Cooper and John [1988]) and evolved into models with "sunspot equilibria" as exemplified in the work, for example, of Farmer and Guo (1994) and Harrison (2005). Models with multiple equilibria typically require either some form of increasing returns or some types of strong complementarities between agents. These complementarities could take many different forms, including increases in investor confidence as more projects are undertaken economy-wide or thick-market search externalities as developed by Diamond (1982).

To illustrate these ideas, we draw on a simple model of positive network externalities developed by Silvestre (2008). Suppose potential investors are ordered on a line segment $(0, K)$ in such a way that their marginal valuations for completing a single project are decreasing. There are positive externalities that depend on the total number of projects, $N < K$. We can think of this, for example, as the value of building a linkage to join a network — with more members, the value to participating in the network increases. Assume that the marginal valuation function for an investor n is given by:

$$P = (K - n)N \qquad (1)$$

Recall that investors are ordered with decreasing valuations. Thus, if the marginal investor will be the Nth investor, and her marginal valuation will be given by:

$$P = (K - N)N \qquad (2)$$

We can solve for N, the number of completed projects, in terms of the marginal valuation P that makes the last person indifferent to completing her project. By construction, all investors $n < N$ have higher valuations and will complete their projects if the Nth person does. Assuming there is a constant marginal cost in completing a project, then the equilibrium number of projects can be illustrated as in Fig. 2.1.

There are three equilibria in the model. First, if $N = 0$, all valuations are zero and no one will want to join the network; thus O is an equilibrium at the origin. The other two equilibria, A and B, occur where the marginal cost curve intersects the marginal valuation function. The equilibrium at A, however, is unstable. To see this, note that as N increases slightly from A, the value to participants would exceed marginal cost and the reverse would be true if N fell. Essentially, at A, the value of extra participants to the network outweighs the decrease in marginal valuation of bringing in the next member to the network. This pattern continues until point B. Past B, the marginal value of additional participation is less than the decrease in marginal valuation from the next member.

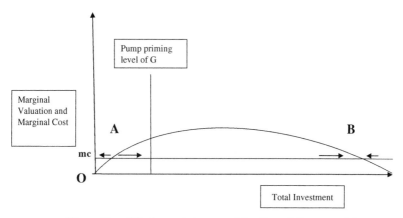

Three Equilibria — A is unstable, O and B are stable.
Government investment can help jump to new equilibrium.

Figure 2.1:   Multiple equilibrium model.

As a result, the two stable equilibria are at B (high participation) and O (no participation).

Now suppose initially that the economy was operating above A and moving slowly to B, but a shock hits the economy and decreases the number of projects below A. The economy would then move towards the no participation equilibrium at O. The government could temporarily halt the decline by providing an autonomous demand for participation at a level exceeding A, as depicted in the diagram. Once the economy is "shocked" to that new position, the economy would resume its path towards the high participation equilibrium and the government could withdraw from the market.

Although the model was specialized, the basic intuition is general. In cases in which there are multiple equilibrium, fiscal policy can act to direct the economy towards a higher-value equilibrium. The economy can be guided to a new stable equilibrium with policies that just are in effect long enough to shift the economy's trajectory. These policies can then be withdrawn without any lasting damage.

A Disappearing Consensus

The apparent consensus behind an aggressive fiscal policy for the United States broke apart in January of 2009 as the details of President Obama's stimulus policy began to be revealed and was passed into law in February. Some of the reasons for the dismantling of the consensus were based on economic factors and some were more politically-based.

Some Chicago economists simply dismissed the stimulus as another reincarnation of Keynesian economics which they had rejected many years ago.[6] Except for the severity of the recession, nothing had changed to bring the Keynesian model back to life. Other critics, however, accepted the underlying demand management rationale, but focused on the difficulty of making timely investments.

---

[6] See Cochrane (2009).

Experts concurred with this assessment, with President Obama's advisors having to argue that the recession would persist for many years to justify the program.[7] Some of the actual policies proposed for increased government spending — e.g. weatherization of housing — neither had the obvious linkages to other sectors of the economy, nor had the type of network externalities which a pump-priming analysis would require. Other projects, such as computerizing medical records and other new technology ventures, could potentially have network linkages but could also have disastrous consequences if implemented too quickly and without a comprehensive plan. Congress also increased "tax expenditures", spending programs implemented through changes in the tax code. While these programs often had the positive, political gloss of tax reductions, many of them — for example, credits for energy research — were ill-defined and likely to have minimal effects on marginal incentives to invest. The Obama administration, with the backing of a liberal coalition, embraced increase in government spending if it was consistent with its long-run goals — even if the actual spending might not come for a number of years and have little to do with pure stabilization policy. Moreover, the specter of increasing debt by nearly $2 trillion on the heels of a financial crisis brought on by too much debt unsettled other observers and raised questions about future inflation and the long-run viability of the U.S. dollar.

Politically, different issues emerged. Predictability, Republicans wanted more tax cuts and envisioned the end game of the stimulus package as permanently higher spending. They succeeded during the negotiations in increasing the share of the stimulus package in the form of tax cuts. The "reversal" problem became a political issue, as subsidies for education and training, for example, were not easily designed to be unwound. In addition, the type of spending included in the package was often in the areas that Republicans had systematically battled against with the Democrats for many years,

---

[7] The Congressional Budget Office (2009). Projections indicate that the full stimulus will take many years.

for example, increases in grants to states for expansions of Medicaid. Finally, the tensions inherent in aid to the states became evident. States could certainly spend money quickly and perhaps avoid their own budgetary reductions triggered by balance-budget requirements, but the potential moral hazard of bailing out profligate state governments (e.g. California) also began to become apparent.

Where does this leave the state of activist fiscal policy? While the strong consensus has faded, the other weapons in the arsenal — alternative forms of monetary or credit policies — cannot always be counted on to be effective in stimulating demand. A clearer distinction between pump-priming policies and policies that just shift aggregate demand would be helpful both in the economic and political context. In the economic context, it could suggest research as to where temporary spending actions might be the most productive. In the political context, it would be useful in drawing a line between policies that truly stimulate and those that are really driven by desires for government growth and not just stabilization. The Obama administration inherited a situation in which discretionary fiscal policy had been given an unusual opportunity to prove itself. Unfortunately, there is a substantial risk that an ill-conceived and politically-oriented stimulus package may not only prove to be ineffective but also end the temporary intellectual reprieve that had been awarded to fiscal policy.

References

Alesina, A. and G. Tabellini (1990). A Positive Theory of Fiscal Deficits and Government Debt. *Review of Economic Studies*, 57, pp. 403–414.

Auerbach, A. (2003). Is There a Role for Discretionary Fiscal Policy. In *Rethinking Stabilization Policy*, Federal Reserve Bank of Kansas City, pp. 109–150.

Barro, R. J. (1974). Are Government Bonds Net Wealth. *Journal of Political Economy*, 82(6), pp. 1095–1117.

Blanchard, O. (1981). Output, the Stock Market, and Interest Rates. *American Economic Review*, pp. 132–143.

Blinder, A. S. (2004). The Case Against the Case Against Discretionary Fiscal Policy. CEPS Working Paper 100.

Blinder A. S. and R. M. Solow (1974). Analytical Foundations of Fiscal Policy. In A. S. Blinder (ed.), *The Economics of Public Finance*, Washington, D.C.: The Brookings Institution.

Carville, J., quoted in http://www.global-investor.com/quote/3497/ James-Carville

Cochrane, J. (2009). Fiscal Stimulus, Fiscal Inflation, or Fiscal Fallacy, available at http://faculty.chicagogsb.edu/john.cochrane/research/Papers/fiscal2.htm

Cooper, R. and A. John (1988). Coordinating Coordination Failures in Keynesian Models. *Quarterly Journal of Economics*, 103, pp. 441–463.

Confucius Biography at http://www.ct.taipei.gov.tw/EN/01-history/hst2.html.

Congressional Budget Office (2009). Estimate available at http://www.cbo.gov/ftpdocs/99xx/doc9968/hr1.pdf

Diamond, P. (1984). Aggregate Demand Management in Search Equilibrium. *Journal of Political Economy*, 90, pp. 881–894.

Eackler, M. (2009). Japan's Big Works Stimulus Is Lesson for U.S. New York Times. (6 February 2009).

Elmendorf, D. and J. Furman (2008). If, When, How: A Primer on Fiscal Stimulus. *The Hamilton Project*. Washington, D.C.: The Brookings Institution.

Farmer, R. E. A. and J. T. Guo (1994). Real Business Cycles and the Animal Spirits Hypothesis. *Journal of Economic Theory*, pp. 42–74.

Feldstein, M. (2009). An $800 Billion Mistake. (29 January), Washington Post, p. A19.

Giavazzi, F. and M. Pagano (1990). Can Severe Fiscal Contractions be Expansionary? Tales of Two Small European Countries. O. In Blanchard and S. Fischer (eds.), *NBER Macroeconomics Annual*, Cambridge, Ma: MIT Press.

Harrison, S. (2005). Do Sunspots Reflect Consumer Confidence: An Empirical Investigation. *Eastern Economic Journal,* 31(1), pp. 55–73.

Hoover, K. D. and S. M. Sheffrin (1992). Causation, Spending, and Taxes: Sand in the Sandbox or Tax Collector for the Welfare State? *American Economic Review*, 82, pp. 225–248.

Krugman, P. (1998). It's Baack: Japan's Slump and the Return of the Liquidity Trap. *Brookings Papers on Economic Activity*, 2, pp. 137–205. Washington, D.C: The Brookings Institution.

Kuttner, K. N. and A. S. Posen (2001). The Great Recession: Lessons for Macroeconomic Policy from Japan. *Brookings Papers on Economic Activity*, 2, pp. 93–160, Washington, D.C: The Brookings Institution.

O'Sullivan, A. M., S. M. Sheffrin and S. J. Perez (2009). *Economics: Principles, Applications and Tools*, 6th ed. Upper Saddle River, New Jersey: Prentice Hall.

Romer, D. H. and C. D. Romer (2007a). The Macroeconomic Effects of Tax Changes: Estimates Based on a New Measure of Fiscal Shocks. NBER Working Paper 13264.

Romer, D. H. and C. D. Romer (2007b). Do Tax Cuts Starve the Beast: The Effects of Tax Changes on Government Spending. NBER Working Paper 13548.

Sheffrin, S. M. (1996). *Rational Expectations*, 2nd Ed., Cambridge and New York: Cambridge University Press.

Silvestre, J. (2008). Note 2 on Externalities of Lecture Notes in Public Finance. Unpublished.

Slemrod, J. and M. Shapiro (2008). Consumer Response to Tax Rebates. *American Economic Review*, 93(1), pp. 381–396.

Uchitelle, L. (2009). Economists Warm to Spending but Debate its Form. (7 January), *New York Times*, p. B1.

CHAPTER 3

The Global Financial Tsunami: Implications for East Asian Economies

TAN KONG YAM

Introduction

The global financial crisis, with its epicenter in the US, has spread across the world since August 2007. It has resulted in unprecedented wealth destruction, the greatest collapse in world output since the 1930s, and continued rise in unemployment and social political dislocation.

This paper analyzes the causes of the crisis, its rapid spread around the world, and particularly its impact on the East and Southeast Asian countries. More significantly, based on existing development in the first half of 2009, this paper attempts to peer into the future to examine the evolving new dynamics between the US and China in the post-crisis environment. Their complex competitive and cooperative dynamics would significantly determine the contours of the new global financial architecture and the international monetary system.

Causes of the Global Financial Crisis

While the causes of the global financial crisis are hotly debated, it is increasingly clear that the collapse of the biggest asset bubble in the post-war era was the result of overly loose credit over a sustained period. As indicated in Fig. 3.1, it was fed by very low interest rates and loose monetary policy of the US Federal Reserve after 2001. Chairman Alan Greenspan, in combating the bursting of the technology bubble in 2001, kept the Fed funds rate at an unprecedented low of below two percent for the period 2002–2005.

In addition, the lack of proper prudential supervision and regulation on mortgages and financial intermediations resulted in reckless lending and over-leveraged financial institutions.

A bubble started to form in the housing market as home prices across the US rose significantly after 2002 (Fig. 3.2). Extensive vested interests in the financial sector were involved. Lobbyists worked hard to prevent legislation intended to restrict predatory lending.

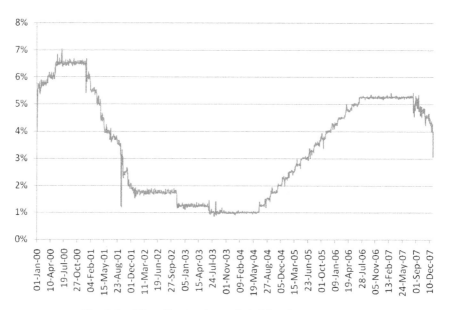

Fig. 3.1:   The effective (actual) fed funds rate was cut.

Source: Federal Reserve.

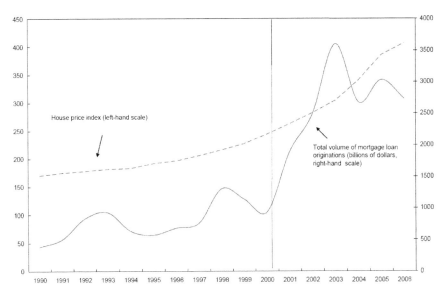

Fig. 3.2:   House prices and credit boom.

Source: CEIC.

Over-valuation of residential real estate was in the interests of the financial institutions doing the lending and securitization of mortgages. Bonuses in Wall Street were tied to the increasing profit of the industry. The enormous fees for rating agencies were also an incentive not to spoil the party while the going was good for everybody.

An important development that led to the unanticipated severity of the financial collapse was the expansion of the shadow banking system, outside of the regulatory system. Due to greater regulation of the formal banking system over the past two decades, most of the financial intermediation has occurred in the shadow banking system. These included the SIVs (special investment vehicles) and conduits, broker's dealers, hedge funds, private equity funds, money market funds and non-bank mortgage lenders. They mostly borrowed short and lent long and in illiquid ways. More significantly, they were highly leveraged, some to the tune of 30 to 1, laying the seed of financial fragility when asset bubbles eventually burst.

As they were not banks, they were more lightly or not regulated at all. They did not have access to deposit insurance and the lender of last resort support from the Fed. Consequently, they were more susceptible to self-fulfilling bank runs as a result of illiquidity. It is also noteworthy that financial engineering often aimed at circumventing regulations. It was partly the result of regulatory arbitrage that created the shadow banking system.

With the benefit of hindsight, excessive leverage or credit obtained for investment purposes lie at the core of the financial crisis. It was excessive leverage that turned large financial institutions into ninepins and key sources of instability and major systemic risks in an unregulated financial system.

In addition, rapid and extensive amount of financial innovations created a financial system much more opaque, complex and non-transparent. Securitization of mortgages led to proliferation of exotic, complex and illiquid assets. By mid 2008, over 60 percent of all US mortgages were securitized. Mortgages were pooled together to form mortgage-backed securities. The income streams from these securities were further tranched to offer income streams of different risk level to different investors commensurate with their risk appetite. However, this "originate and distribute" model of mortgage financing led to the lack of incentive by the loan originators to monitor the performance of the mortgages. Hence securitization as well as globalization of the financial markets led to increasing complexity, financial fragility and connectedness between financial institutions, both within and across countries.

The rise in extreme free market ideology since the Thatcher and Reagan revolution in the early 1980s has also provided the backdrop. The strong prevailing belief was in the self-equilibrating and self-healing powers of the laissez faire capitalism, rather than the inherent instability of the market economy and the need to have a vigilant and prudential regulatory authority to prevent the financial system and capitalist economy from running off the rails.

This extreme free market ideology served the major vested interests well. The globalization of the financial market allowed the most competitive US financial industry to press for extensive financial liberalization on the rest of the world. Lighter regulation and taxation enhanced global capital's profitability. The financial industry grew to represent an unprecedented share of 25 percent in the US stock market capitalization and over 35 percent of corporate profit.

Consequently, increasing optimism, under-estimation of risk as well as the lack of proper regulations were the key factors leading to this significant increase in the leverage ratio of financial institutions. During the period of rising prosperity and increasing asset prices, higher leverage led to increasing rate of return to capital. However, as the value of assets went into decline or became more uncertain, the higher the leverage, the greater is the probability that capital could be totally wiped out, the higher is the probability that financial institutions would become insolvent.

The proximate cause of the financial crisis is the excessive lending of the sub-prime mortgage market and the housing bubble. Rising housing prices led to increasingly lax lending practices. In addition, households resorted to extensive over-borrowing to sustain their consumption spending even though their real wages have been stagnating. Taking advantage of rising home value, they extracted equity value out of their home mortgages, essentially treating their home as an ATM machine. This rising private consumption expenditure generated by mortgage-equity withdrawal is estimated to have added an additional average rate of two percentage points to GDP growth for each of the year during the period 2002–2006. Consequently, when the housing bubble burst, the over-borrowed household sector's tattered balance sheets were starkly revealed.

As domestic savings rate in the US was low and falling, a significant portion of the over-borrowing by US households and financial institutions as well as the government sector was financed by foreigners, especially foreign central banks. As indicated in Figs. 3.3 and 3.4, US was by far the largest borrower, accounting for 49.4 percent of total global capital import, followed by Spain (9.3 percent), UK (9.1 percent) and Australia (3.4 percent). The largest capital exporters were China (21.4 percent), Japan

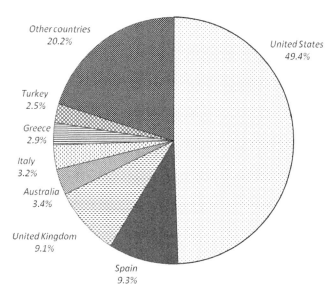

Fig. 3.3:   Major net importers of capital in 2007.

Source: IMF.

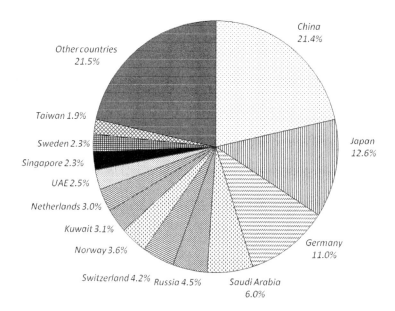

Fig. 3.4:   Major net exporters of capital in 2007.

Source: IMF.

(12.6 percent), Germany (11.0 percent), Saudi Arabia (6.0 percent) and Russia (4.5 percent).

Collapse of the Housing Bubble and Trigger of the Crisis

The excesses of mortgage lending became evident when housing prices peaked in 2006 and some sub-prime mortgage lenders started to declare bankruptcy in March 2007 when home prices began to decline (Fig. 3.5).

The initial assessment of the Federal Reserve was that the sub prime crisis would be isolated and contained. It was estimated that total losses on U.S. sub-prime loans and securities, as of October 2007, was about $250 billion dollars, a manageable loss that could be absorbed by the financial institutions.

However, the collapse in housing prices spread rapidly among the financial institutions and to other markets. The financial fragility resulting from the securitization of mortgage-backed assets as well as the over-leveraged shadow banking system was seriously under-estimated. The largest mortgage originator,

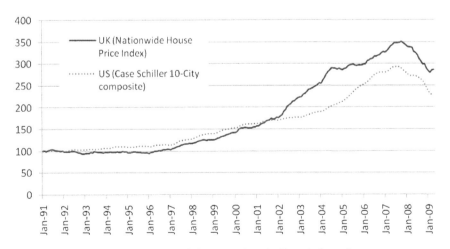

Fig. 3.5:   US & UK house prices indices (rebased).

Source: Thomson Datastream and Standard & Poor's.

Countrywide Financial, collapsed and had to be acquired. Highly-leveraged hedge funds and other financial institutions with mortgage-backed securities saw their balance sheets severely mauled by the collapse in asset prices.

Confidence in the creditworthiness of many financial institutions was totally shaken. Inter-bank lending became disrupted. In September 2008, as a result of the disorderly collapse of Lehman Brothers, the financial system went through a cardiac seizure and the whole financial system actually underwent a total meltdown. The generalized uncertainty resulted in panic and a run. There was great uncertainty about the amount of toxic assets out there, who was holding it and hence a collapse of trust. Risk aversion skyrocketed and there was massive panic and a rush to liquidity.

Credit spreads or the risk premium over the risk-free rate of interest widened to unprecedented levels. In particular, the spread between three-month Libor and the three-month overnight index swap (OIS), a measure of risk and illiquidity effect, rose very substantially in September 2008, indicating a significant increase in counter-party risks (see Fig. 3.6).

Originally, securitization was hailed to spread risk to those who could best bear it and hence, enhance the resilience of the financial system. It turned out that with the complexity of the securitized assets being more opaque and hence difficult to value, the increase in uncertainty actually became larger, leading to rising perceived risk of insolvency and higher probability of a run on these institutions. Moreover, the larger leverage which led to less capital relative to assets at the outset aggravated the fragility of the system and increased the probability of insolvency, leading to greater fear and higher probability of a run.

In addition, as the financial institutions in the advanced countries faced a credit crunch, they were forced to cut the credit lines of their subsidiaries in the emerging markets. These cuts resulted in the reduction of credit to domestic borrowers in the emerging markets and the forced sale of assets. This linkage was an important channel whereby the financial crisis was transmitted rapidly from the advanced countries to the emerging markets.

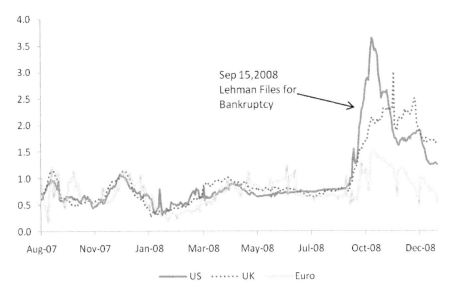

Fig. 3.6: LIBOR-OIS spread: 3-month Libor rate minus overnight index swap (in percent).

Source: Thomson Datastream.

With the financial system in serious crisis, the authority undertook an unprecedented measure of resuscitating the financial system.

Through zero interest rates, quantitative and credit easing, the purchase of private and public debts, recapitalization, liquidity support, guarantees and insurance, the Federal Reserve injected ever larger quantities of money into the system. Within a couple of weeks, the balance sheet of the Federal Reserve ballooned from US$800 billion to US$1,800 billion. It was also strongly committed to the tune of US$12 trillion to the financial system, to support major financial institutions and prevent them from failing and triggering further crisis (Figs. 3.7 and 3.8).

Fortunately, the unprecedented measures have stabilized the financial system. By early 2009, the financial crisis showed signs of abating. Credit spreads have declined, and inter-bank lending gradually resumed. A catastrophic global financial crisis was narrowly averted.

46   *Tan Kong Yam*

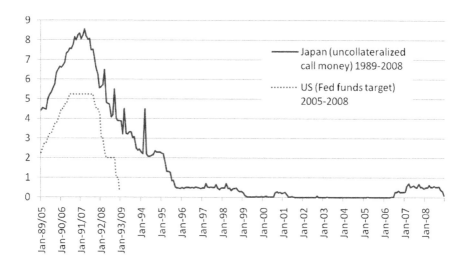

Fig. 3.7: Central bank policy rates (in percent).

Source: Thomson Datastream.

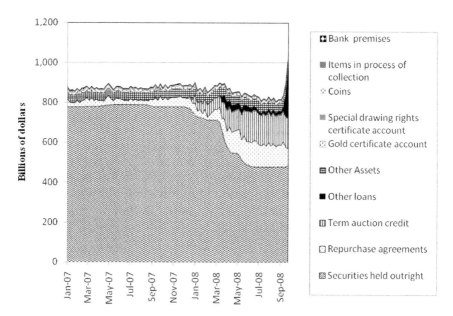

Fig. 3.8: Components of the asset side of the Federal Reserve balance sheet (4 Jan, 2007–25 Sep, 2008).

Source: Federal Reserve.

Impact on Asian Economies

With its extensive trade, financial, investment and production linkages with the US economy, the Asian countries were confronted with an unprecedented challenge from the US financial crisis.

Fortunately, the financial sector of the Asian countries has managed to weather the global financial crisis relatively well. Bank credits continued to flow to businesses and household sectors normally. As indicated in Table 3.1, the growth of private domestic banking credit continued to be largely sustained or even expanded more rapidly throughout the four quarters of 2008, compared to the earlier pre-crisis period of 2006–07.

This sustained credit expansion was due to the fact that the Asian financial institutions have had limited exposure to the sub-prime and toxic assets of the US. In addition, since the 1997–98 Asian financial crisis, the banking sector in the Asian countries has undergone serious restructuring with enhanced resilience.

According to the estimates of Kawai, Lamberte and Yang (2008), the direct exposure of the Asian financial institutions to sub-prime financial assets and instruments was minimal. As of May 2008, total sub-prime losses amounted to US$19.5 billion in Asia compared to US$157.7 billion in the US. Measured as a share of total

Table 3.1:   Growth of private domestic banking credit.

	2006	2007	2008 Q1	2008 Q2	2008 Q3	2008 Q4
China, People's Rep. of	12.1	18.0	19.1	16.9	14.8	13.2
Hong Kong, China	4.3	7.6	9.6	14.6	18.3	0.6[a]
India	28.1	22.8	22.4	24.2	24.8	27.8[a]
Indonesia	13.9	18.9	27.4	31.5	34.2	36.5
Korea, Rep. of	10.8	14.3	14.3	16.0	16.2	16.4[b]
Malaysia	8.6	9.0	10.9	10.8	9.7	9.5[a]
Philippines	1.2	5.9	8.4	8.9	16.9	16.5
Singapore	3.6	10.2	18.5	20.5	20.7	17.5
Thailand	6.4	3.3	5.4	6.8	9.5	9.7

[a] October and November 2008. [b] October 2008. [c] Shading indicates a deterioration.
Source: Asian Development Bank.

Table 3.2:   Estimated Asian sub-prime losses.

	United States	Japan	Korea Rep. of	China People's Rep. of	Malaysia	Total Asia
Subprime losses ($ billion)	157.7	8.7	0.4	2.8	0.1	19.5
Total bank assets ($ billion)	15,492	11,350	1,184	5,950	267	20,965
Capital of banks ($ billion)	1,572	572	85	256	29	998
Subprime losses as share of capital (%)	10.03	1.52	0.52	1.08	0.30	1.95
Subprime losses as share of assets (%)	1.02	0.08	0.04	0.05	0.03	0.09

Source: Kawai, Lamberte and Yang.

capital among Asian banks, these losses amounted to 1.95 percent compared to the US ratio of 10.03 percent (see Table 3.2).

As a result of extensive restructuring of the banking sector after the Asian financial crisis in 1997–98, the Asian banking system has been put on a sound footing. As indicated in Table 3.3, non-performing loans ratio has fallen to a low single-digit level in most of the countries. Risk-weighted capital-adequacy ratio has risen to the mid-teens and the return on assets has improved substantially from 1999 after the crisis period.

In addition, there was no corresponding shadow banking system which was outside the regulatory system of the formal banking system emerging in the Asian countries. This absence of the over-leveraged and lightly or not regulated financial intermediation saved the Asian banking system from the fragility inflicted on the US financial system.

Consequently, when the global financial crisis hit the Asian countries, their banking system was able to withstand the shock well. Bank credits continue to flow to the private sector in support of business investment and household lending. The real sector of the economy was not hit by the credit crunch as had happened in the US and EU countries.

More significantly, Asian banks have not relied on foreign borrowings to finance their loans, after the painful lesson of the Asian financial crisis. As at end of 2008, foreign liabilities to domestic

Table 3.3: Indicators of financial soundness in Asian banks.

Developing Asia	Non-performing loans (% of bank loans)		Risk-weighted capital-adequacy ratio		Banks' return on assets	
	1999	2007 or 2008	1999	2007 or 2008	1999	2007 or 2008
China, People's Rep. of	–	6.7	12.8	7.7	0.1	1.0
Hong Kong, China	7.2	1.2	18.7	14.3	0.4	2.0
India	14.7	2.4	11.2	12.6	0.5	1.0
Indonesia	32.9	8.5	−6.7	16.8	−8.7	2.3
Korea, Rep.of	8.3	0.8	10.8	12.0	−1.3	0.9
Malaysia	11.0	2.2	12.5	12.6	0.7	1.5
Philippines	13.6	3.9	17.5	15.9	0.4	1.4
Singapore	5.3	1.8	20.6	14.0	1.2	1.4
Thailand	38.6	5.3	12.4	14.8	−5.7	0.1
Others						
Japan	5.8	1.5	11.9	12.3	−0.9	0.3
United States	2.2	5.1	12.2	12.8	1.3	0.6

Source: Asian Development Bank.

deposits ranged from a low 0.01 in China, 0.04 in Thailand, 0.07 in Indonesia, 0.11 in Malaysia to 0.30 in Korea. Consequently, the credit crunch gripping the banking system in the US and Europe did not cause any liquidity problem in the Asian banking system.

However, some of the weaker Asian economies were hit by the withdrawal of external finance and the deterioration of investor confidence. For example, in Korea, small and medium enterprises were particularly affected by the reduction in lending by the banks as risk aversion increased. In addition, as investors from the developed countries pulled back from the developing countries to bolster their balance sheets at home, tighter external finance and the rise in risk premium had also affected the raising of funds by Indonesia, Vietnam and the Philippines.

While the banking system in the Asian countries has remained sound and has managed to shield them from the calamitous effect of the credit crunch in the developed countries, the supporting measures of the monetary authorities of the Asian countries in bolstering the financial markets and systems have also greatly helped in maintaining stability and sustaining confidence. These measures have included liquidity injection, widening the range of assets that could be used as collateral, expansion of deposit guarantees as well as currency swaps arrangements with the central banks of major industrial countries.

The greatest negative impact of the global financial crisis on the Asian countries is through the channel of trade and external demand. East and Southeast Asian countries have traditionally employed an outward-oriented export development strategy to industrialize. Consequently, their exports to GDP ratio have been among the highest in the world (see Fig. 3.9). The decline in GDP of the US, EU and Japan has resulted in a sharp contraction of the developing Asian countries' exports.

As indicated in Figs. 3.10 and 3.11, the collapse in export and import growth has been unprecedented, falling from the pre-crisis level of 20–30 percent increase in 2008 to the negative 30–50 percent by the first quarter of 2009. The decline was particularly serious for

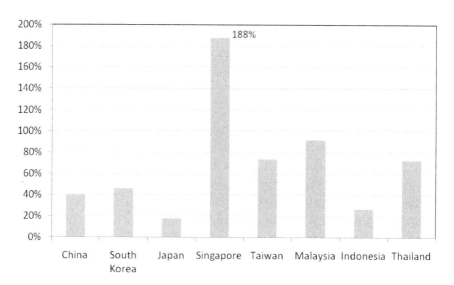

Fig. 3.9:   East Asia: Exports as percentage of GDP, 2007.

Source: CEIC.

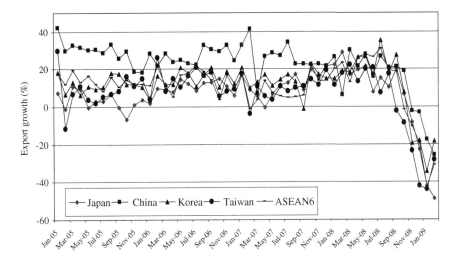

Fig. 3.10: Export growth of Japan, China, Korea, Taiwan and ASEAN6 (Jan 2005–Mar 2009).

Source: CEIC.

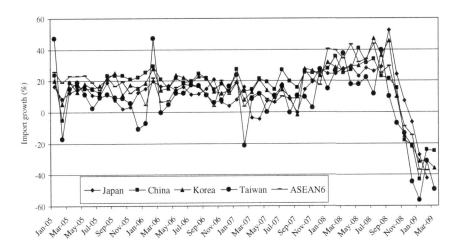

Fig. 3.11: Import growth of Japan, China, Korea, Taiwan and ASEAN6 (Jan 2005–Mar 2009).

Source: CEIC.

electronic products, which has been the fastest increasing component of Asian exports to the US and EU.

In addition, while international production fragmentation over the past 15 years has resulted in the rapid increase in intra-regional trade, estimates conducted by the Asian Development Bank have indicated that only about one-third of the final demand generated from these intra-regional trades came from Asian countries while the other two-thirds have originated from the final demand of the western industrial economies. Consequently, when external demands from the western industrial economies collapsed, the extensive intra-regional trade within Asia also declined substantially. This revealed the serious weakness of the Asian region, where final demand of private consumption and investments has been too weak to generate growth momentum within the region. The dependence of the Asian countries on external demand from the western countries was plainly revealed by this unprecedented collapse in exports.

The collapse of exports resulted in numerous factory closures and layoffs across the region, particularly in the electronics and light manufacturing industries. The resulting increase in unemployment led to decline in domestic consumption and falling consumer confidence. The knock-on effect was the decline in private investment in these industries as well as the collapse in demand for capital goods.

Consequently, GDP is projected to contract significantly in most Asian countries in 2009 and only gradually recover by 2010 (Table 3.4). In particular, the heavily manufactured export-dependent economies like the NIEs are projected to contract significantly in 2009, especially for Singapore (–7.5 percent), Taiwan (–9.3 percent), Korea (–10.1 percent), Malaysia (–3.0 percent) and Thailand (–4.4 percent). Only China with its massive fiscal stimulus in domestic demand is projected to grow by 6–7 percent in 2009.

To combat the regional collapse in exports, the fall in GDP and the rise in unemployment, the regional central banks rapidly eased credit to ensure adequate liquidity. As indicated in Fig. 3.12, policy rates were cut by 100 to 700 basis points between

Table 3.4: Projected GDP Growth for 2009–10.

Country	2009		2010
China	7.0*	6.0**	6.5*
Japan	–	−6.4	–
Hong Kong	−2.0	−5.9	8.6
Korea	−3.0	−10.1	4.0
Singapore	−5.0	−7.5	3.5
Taiwan	−4.0	−9.3	2.4
Indonesia	3.6	1.9	5.0
Malaysia	−0.2	−3.0	4.4
Philippines	2.5	−1.9	3.5
Thailand	−2.0	−4.4	3.0

Sources: * Asian Development Bank, March 31, 2009.
　　　　** Economist.Com/Country Briefings, April 19, 2009.

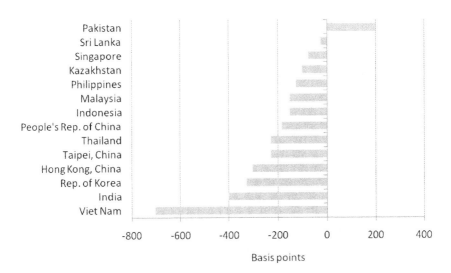

Fig. 3.12: Changes in policy rates from 30 September 2008 to 16 March 2009.
Sources: Census and Economic Information Center, Asian Development Bank.

September 2008 to March 2009 in most of the Asian countries to stimulate the economy.

In addition to monetary stimulus, the governments of the Asian countries implemented substantial package of fiscal stimulus to

Table 3.5: Impact of fiscal stimulus packages in developing Asia (simulation).

Economy	Package as share of 2009 GDP (%)	Impact on GDP (% change from baseline)		
		2009	2010	2011
China, People's Rep. of	1.2	1.3	2.0	1.5
Hong Kong, China	1.4	1.1	0.5	0.3
India	1.6	0.5	0.3	0.3
Indonesia	1.3	1.3	0.8	0.4
Korea, Rep. of	2.5	1.6	1.2	1.0
Malaysia	2.6	3.1	4.1	1.5
Philippines	4.1	2.4	3.5	1.7
Singapore	5.9	3.6	2.8	0.4
Taipei, China	2.1	1.4	1.2	0.7
Thailand	6.4	6.5	7.9	7.4

Sources: Oxford Economics, 2009 and Asian Development Bank.

offset the effect of collapse in external demand. In particular, China announced an early major stimulus package of Rmb 4 trillion in November 2008 to stimulate domestic demand to offset the collapse in external demand.

As indicated in Table 3.5, these stimulus packages amounted to 1.2 to 6.4 percent of GDP. The stimulus package measured as a share of GDP was particularly large for Thailand (6.4 percent), Singapore (5.9 percent), Philippines (4.1 percent), Malaysia (2.6 percent), Korea (2.5 percent), and Taiwan (2.1 percent). They are expected to raise GDP growth from the baseline case by a substantial amount to neutralize the effect of the fall in external demand.

More significantly, the crisis has resulted in greater cooperation among the East and Southeast Asian countries. In May 2009, the Association of Southeast Asian Nations (ASEAN) and its three Asian dialogue partners, Japan, China and South Korea, formally established a liquidity crisis fund worth US$120 billion. This Chiang Mai Initiative Multilateralization (CMIM) was designed to provide ASEAN+3 members rapid support to bolster their foreign exchange rates during times of serious liquidity shortages and capital outflows.

The CMIM was designed as a major expansion of the older Chiang Mai Initiative (CMI), a series of 16 bilateral currency swaps established in the aftermath of the Asian financial crisis, when the falling Thai Baht triggered a domino effect of financial and economic collapse throughout the region in 1997.

The CMIM represented a delicate power balance in the region. Japan and China (plus Hong Kong) each contributed US$38.4 billion to the fund. The program also received US$24 billion from South Korea, US$4.76 billion each from Indonesia, Malaysia, Singapore and Thailand, US$3.68 billion from the Philippines, US$1 billion from Vietnam, and smaller amounts from Brunei, Cambodia, Laos and Myanmar. The fund reflected a deep desire among the East Asian countries to wean itself from over-dependence on and subordination to the Western-dominated financial system. After all, the memory of the severe restructuring requirements of the IMF that put borrowing governments at risk of political backlash, especially in Indonesia and Thailand, were still fresh. By contrast, the new CMIM scheme will be made available in accordance with criteria established by the ASEAN+3 member states, aimed at providing bridging funds over the short term. Consequently, it will be managed with sensitivity towards the specific characteristics of the borrowing countries and designed to keep the current system intact, avoiding the need for drastic financial and economic restructuring and social political dislocation.

For the past decade, over-borrowing and over-consuming countries like the US, UK, Australia and New Zealand have been the consumers of first and last resort in the global economy. Their resulting current account deficits have supported the expansion in export and current account surplus of Asian countries like China, Japan and Korea and other Southeast Asian countries as well as Germany. With the global financial crisis, deficit countries would need to retrench and reduce their current account deficits to rebalance their economies. Consequently, the export-driven model of development of the Asian countries would face increasing difficulties in garnering external demand to drive their economies. Alternative locomotives would need to be harnessed to generate future growth.

Future Trends

A critical issue after the global financial crisis is the new sources of growth for the Asian developing countries, particularly China. The traditional model of export-oriented development strategy is hitting its limit. Asia countries, particularly China, can no longer depend on external demand and the consumption of first and last resort of the US consumers to sustain their future growth. A more balanced model of growth, with greater dependence on domestic and regional consumption and investments, would need to be found to sustain future growth of the Asian countries over the medium and longer term.

At the fundamental level, the global imbalance over the past six years was basically due to the imbalances between US and China. Savings rate in China has risen enormously, leading to rising current account surplus that reached almost 10 percent of GDP by 2008. Policies for rebalancing would need to address the sustained high savings and the corresponding weakness in private consumption expenditure in China. A significant contributing factor to the rising saving rate in China is the rise in corporate saving, largely reflecting the retained earnings of firms, especially the SOEs. Policies that could reduce corporate savings include higher dividend payout to the central government which can then be recycled into greater budgetary spending on health care, education and social security expenditure to boost domestic demand as well as reduce household burden and hence increase private consumer spending. In addition, rising corporate savings is also partly due to subsidized low interest rates, low land and resource and energy prices. Raising these factor prices would reduce corporate savings especially for SOEs, improve returns to household savings and boost consumption, increase government revenue from land and resources which can then be recycled back to the household sector through greater budgetary spending on education, health care, low-cost housing, social safety net provisions and old age pension support. This would greatly ease household burden and reduce the need for precautionary savings and enhance private consumptions expenditure. These policies would promote a more harmonious society as envisaged by the Hu-Wen regime and put the welfare of the people first in its development strategy. They would also improve income distribution in the urban areas, reduce rural-urban inequality, coastal inland disparity as well as reduce environmental degradation.

Historically, sustained benign economic environment and expansion often leads to credit boom and speculative bubbles. Borrowers and lenders looked at historical performance and the low risk level and become too optimistic about the future and under-estimate the risk inherent in investments. The period between the mid-1980s till 2008 was a period of great moderation, low inflation rate, low interests rates and good economic growth and sustained bull run in the stock markets globally All these led to severe under-estimation of risk, resulting in over-leverage, over-borrowing and over-lending of the household and financial sector.

For the past 20 years, the savings rate of the US economy has been declining. The country has been consuming more than it has been producing. This continuous process of living beyond its means has resulted in the accumulation of debt, largely by the household and financial sectors.

At the most fundamental level, the epicenter of this global financial crisis is the US. It is caused by excessive over-consumption and over-borrowing by the household sector, excessive borrowing, excessive leverage and reckless lending by the financial institutions, excessive borrowing of the corporate sector and excessive debt of the public sector. The credit, assets and especially housing bubble created an artificial boom that eventually went bust. Hence, at the most fundamental level, this is a crisis of debt, credit and solvency of the household, corporate and financial sectors of the US economy (Fig. 3.13).

The reckless fiscal policies in the US since 2001 have led to increasingly serious twin fiscal and current account deficits. These resulted from the unsustainable tax cuts, the rising government spending on foreign wars and domestic security as well as the collapse in household savings. The danger is the US is repeating the

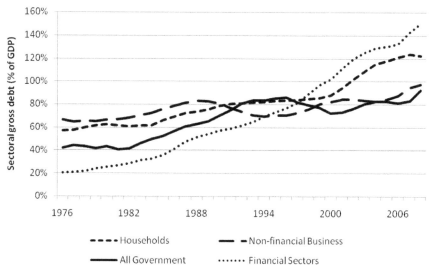

Fig. 3.13:   Debt as a share of GDP (US).

Source: CEIC.

experience of the UK. The decline of the British Empire started after World War II when the enormous costs of the war resulted in the UK becoming a net borrower and a net debtor. This decline from the creditor to a debtor position was an important reason for the steady decline of the British pound as the leading global reserve currency.

Consequently, the financial crisis is not merely a crisis of liquidity. Hence the resolution of this crisis depends on the resolution of the real and financial excesses of the household, corporate and financial sectors that triggered the crisis in the first place. It is likely to be protracted and extremely painful for households and the financial institutions as well as politically contentious.

While the catastrophic financial collapse was averted, the economy has not undergone the necessary de-leveraging and debt-restructuring process. The Federal Reserve has basically taken all the liabilities of the household sector, the banking system and financial institutions, and the corporate sector and socialized all the bad debt and put them in the balance sheet of the government. While it temporarily prevented the financial system from suffering total collapse, it has basically transferred the excesses cumulated by the private sectors over the past two decades into the government balance sheet. Consequently, the major issue will increasingly become the long-run fiscal sustainability of the US government as well as the creditworthiness and long-run solvency of the US government.

The socialization of private debt will significantly increase the public debt burden. In the US, the CBO has estimated that public debt to GDP ratio would rise substantially from 40 percent to 80 percent over the next several years. The IMF projected that debt as a share of GDP of the US would increase from pre-crisis projection of 63.4 percent to 81.2 percent in 2009 and rise significantly to reach 97.3 percent by 2012. In addition, the rise in public debt is likely to lead to an increase in long-term interest rates and the debt-service burden, further putting pressure on the trend-increase in future public debt.

The servicing of the debt burden will necessitate the politically painful process of increases in taxes, the trimming of government spending as well as the possibility of using inflationary tax to erode the real value of public debt. The resulting increase in political conflict and class tension will be substantial.

Given the nature of the US democratic system, and the difficulty for popularly-elected politicians to advocate increase in taxes and cut in spending, the path of least resistance to resolve the public debt issue could increasingly fall on the use of inflationary tax to erode away the real value of the debt. This option is likely to prove increasingly attractive as unlike in the earlier period, the rapid increase in foreign holdings of US public debt over the past decade has led to a situation where almost 60 percent of the total stock of government debt are now being held by foreigners, especially central banks in China, Japan, Russia and the oil-producing states. These countries are mostly strategic rivals or states which are protectorates of the US military and hence more readily targets for an inflationary tax to prevent the default of the US government. In addition, the inflationary environment could also have the advantage of raising housing prices in the US, thus helping to reduce the pressure of collapsing housing prices on the balance sheets of the household and financial sectors and the health of the overall economy. Consequently, over the next decade, the world economy could move towards the performance period of the 1970s where low growth, high inflation, and high and volatile real interest rates resulted in stagflation and rising unemployment.

In addition, the increasing concern on medium-term fiscal sustainability of the US as well as the rising risk that monetization of the fiscal deficits will increasingly become politically necessary, would lead to rising inflationary pressure, increases in nominal and real interest rates. This increase in the interest rates will crowd out private consumption, capital investments, the tentative recovery of the housing sector and result in slow and below potential growth for a sustained period.

More significantly, China would increasingly get tired of financing the US deficit through the purchase of low-yielding US treasuries. With the Rmb expected to continue to appreciate against the US dollar, the holdings of US treasuries will lead to increasing declining value measured in domestic currencies. This shrinkage effect would be compounded by expected rising inflation and declining real yield in these assets. In setting up the China Investment Corporation (CIC), China is trying to shift from the holding of US treasuries into other real assets, including large equity investments and actual control of corporate firms and financial institutions. The controversy over the Unocal–Cnooc political backlash indicates that rising financial protectionism could be an increasing source of tension. The need for the US economy to finance its deficits and the desire for China to have more say in the choice of the form and terms of its financing of the US deficit is likely to be an increasing source of conflict in the future.

China has no choice but to diversify its foreign reserve management. On 10 June 2009, China's State Administration for Foreign Exchange (SAFE) announced the easing of restriction on how Chinese companies use foreign exchange to invest abroad. Beginning August 1, the new regulations will allow a whole range of Chinese companies to use their foreign reserve earned to invest in their subsidiaries abroad or make overseas acquisitions. Taking advantage of the global financial crisis, China has increasingly supported Chinese companies to purchase foreign assets, particularly strategic commodities and advanced technology from international companies who are facing tight liquidity or are in financial difficulties. The easing of foreign exchange reserve investments will loosen the existing centrally–controlled management of the foreign exchange reserves. It will significantly diversify the investments of foreign reserves away from the holding of US government debt into real investments into companies, resources as well as advanced technology. This trend could actually aggravate the global scramble for resources by intensifying the competition for investments in the resource sectors in Africa, Latin America and Australia.

Acquisition of energy resources overseas could be an even more sensitive venture. Over the past several years, China had encouraged its energy companies to branch out overseas and acquire resources via joint ventures or outright purchases of oil and natural gas fields. They were active in Africa, central Asia, Southeast Asia and Latin America. The key focus for most Chinese resource acquisitions abroad were about controlling access to resources from the ground to the Chinese facilities. This was designed to bypass potential interferences in international supplies by giving China control from top to bottom, thus minimizing the potential for any external disruptions.

Australia has been at the forefront of China's resource acquisitions. The Aluminum Corporation of China (Chinalco) has proposed to invest US$19.5 billion in the British–Australian mining conglomerate Rio Tinto. China Minmetals Corp has offered to invest US$1.7 billion in Australia's OZ Minerals Ltd. In addition to backing Chinese companies, the government is looking at taking a more direct role in foreign acquisitions. The China Investment Corp. has begun to focus heavily on future acquisition of resources and other concrete investments rather than on financial investments abroad.

Given the deep mistrust of the West on China's monolithic communist party and the close relationship between business and government, these high-profile acquisitions are likely to provoke substantial political backlash and intensify conflict.

Beijing is also using the China Development Bank (CDB) to gain new resources in return for loans abroad. The CDB has extended a loan of US$10 billion to Brazil's Petroleo Brasileiro SA (Petrobras) for deepwater energy development. The loan will be repaid in oil. In February 2009, China and Russia struck a deal that will give Russian energy firms Transneft a loan of US$10 billion and Rosneft an additional loan of US$15 billion to finance the East Siberian oil field development and production and to connect the Eastern Siberia–Pacific Ocean pipeline to China. In return, China would receive about 300,000 barrels per day of oil for the next 20 years. China has taken advantage of Russia's need to cut a deal out of economic desperation as its state-owned energy firms felt the pain of the global credit crunch, low oil prices and falling demand.

China's actions to further its leadership role in the region included a US$10 billion investment cooperation fund and an offer of US$15 billion in credit to its Southeast Asian neighbors. The credit fund was aimed at helping the weaker countries weather the current global financial crisis. The investment cooperation fund would finance infrastructure development linking China and its neighbors, further enhancing trade and transport linkages. In particular, China has focused on the Greater Mekong sub-region area as a key part of its periphery strategy of cultivating and nurturing neighboring friendship and cooperation. China has also designated its two provinces within the Mekong region, Yunnan and Guangxi, as the key frontline provinces in enhancing linkages and reviving its historical influence in Southeast Asia.

In response to the current international financial and economic crisis, the Chinese government has also made a major strategic decision to enhance the role of the Rmb. As an immature creditor, China has been forced to make its international lending and accumulate her foreign exchange reserves in the US dollar and the Euro. This resulted in significant foreign exchange risk for China. If China was lending to the US and Europe in Rmb, China would be able to continue to run large current account surpluses without taking on as much financial risk as it is now.

During the G20 summit meeting in London in April 2009, Chinese President Hu Jintao met with Russian President Dmitri Medvedev to discuss a plan to create an alternative global reserve currency that could eventually replace the US dollar in global trade. The proposed currency would be based on the IMF's system of Special Drawing Rights.

This followed closely after the governor of the PBC, Zhou Xiaochuan , proposed a scheme for a "super-sovereign reserve currency" in March 2009. His proposed "international currency" sounded very similar to European Currency Unit (ECU), the precursor to the present day Euro. When the ECU was conceived in 1979, it was an artificial currency used by the member states of the European Community as their internal accounting unit. Weights of national currencies in the ECU basket were decided by their trade and GDP as proportions of the EU's totals. After almost 20 years, the ECU eventually evolved into the Euro, the single currency that replaced sovereign currencies inside the Euro zone.

Presently, the value of the current SDR is derived from a basket of currencies including USD, Euro, Yen, and Pound, accounting for 44 percent, 34 percent, 11 percent and 11 percent, respectively.

Zhou's proposal was to include China's RMB as well as other currencies like the Russian Ruble in the SDR currency basket. Some appropriate measure of GDP would be the weighing factor in deciding the currencies' percentage in the basket. Zhou's idea could thus be interpreted as a long-term plan to establish a global currency unit similar to ECU. As the ECU finally developed into the Euro, the new SDR could also become the world's new single currency. This proposal was clearly an attempt by China to gain greater influence in the evolving new international monetary system. It was intended to herald the transition from a US dollar-dominated to a multiple currencies international monetary system.

China has started to make rapid adjustment and policy changes to facilitate the use of the RMB as settlement currency for current account transactions in the Asian region and elsewhere in the world. It has intensified the promotion of the international use of the RMB and accelerated movement toward full RMB convertibility. RMB-denominated lines of credit have been extended to several countries and bilateral local currency swaps have been negotiated with Malaysia, South Korea, Indonesia, Hong Kong, Argentina and Belarus.

There would be downside to the promotion of the Rmb as an international currency. With a fully convertible currency, Beijing would no longer be able to artificially adjust or control the value of the yuan, and hence the international price of its exports to protect its exporters and the hundreds of thousands of jobs they provide. Moreover, having a fully convertible and internationally tradable currency means the yuan would no longer be immune to speculative attacks.

In the short to medium term, Zhou's proposal is not likely to pose any serious challenge to the dominance of the US dollar in the international monetary system. The US government, as custodian of the world's premier reserve currency and largest international debtor country, presently has de-facto veto power within the IMF voting structure. Consequently, the US is unlikely to cooperate, as implementation of Zhou's proposal would greatly diminish the advantages of reserve currency status presently enjoyed by the US. However, over the longer term, if the fiscal sustainability issue in the US becomes of increasing concern among other major industrialized and developing countries as well as the financial markets, a gradual shift of global opinion towards a multiple currency international monetary system could gain greater support and momentum. Alternatively, a very likely scenario could be the gradual fragmentation of the international monetary system into three currency zones, US, Euro and Rmb.

References

Asian Development Bank (2009). *Asian Development Outlook.*

Baily, M., R. Litan and M. Johnson (2008). *The Origins of the Financial Crisis.* Brookings Institution.

Blanchard, O. (2009). The Crisis: Basic Mechanisms and Appropriate Policies. IMP working paper WP/09/80.

International Monetary Fund (2009). *The State of Public Finances: Outlook and Medium term Policies After the 2008 Crisis.*

Kawai, M., M. Lamberte and D. Y. Yang (2008). *Global Shocks, Capital Flows and Asian Regional Economic Cooperation.* Tokyo: Asian Development Bank Institute.

Roubini, N. (2008). The Rising Risk of a Systemic Financial Meltdown, Twelve Steps to Financial Disaster. *RGE Monitor.*

Sachs, J. (2009). Achieving Global Cooperation on Economic Recovery and Long term Sustainable Development. ADB distinguished speakers program.

Taylor, J. (2008). *The Financial Crisis and the Policy Response: An Empirical Analysis and What Went Wrong.* Hoover Institution.

Zhou, X. (2009). *Reform the International Monetary System.*

CHAPTER 4

Global Financial Tsunami: Can the Industrial Relations Mechanism Save Singapore This Time Around?

ROSALIND CHEW

Since independence in 1965, the Singapore economy has weathered three recessions, in 1985, in 1997 and in 2003. During each recession, Singapore used the industrial relations mechanism to get the economy out of the recession and recovery was achieved in good time. However, can the old trick still do the job to get the Singapore economy out of the current global tsunami? This paper will first identify three mechanisms which can help to minimize the impact of a recession and restore employment. It will then examine the nature of each of our past recessions and explain why the industrial relations mechanism was used each time. In the current global financial tsunami, the jobs credit scheme which will be financed by our national reserves has been put up to keep employment from shrinking. The objective of this paper is to analyze the differences between the three previous recessions and the current global financial tsunami, and to ascertain whether we can still use the same old mechanism to get Singapore out of trouble and if, indeed, it did work at all in the first place.

Overview

Singapore is a small and open economy. Her economic growth has been quite satisfactory. One US dollar is worth about 1.50 Sing dollars in 2008 compared to three Sing dollars in the 1960s. The Singapore government has always enjoyed budget surpluses and managed to accumulate a large amount of foreign reserves. Because it is a small open economy which faces cyclical demand for its exports, cyclical unemployment can be a problem. This paper discusses how Singapore avoids cyclical unemployment, which must be prevented at all costs because Singapore does not have an unemployment benefits scheme or even an equivalent.

Converting a Retirement Scheme into a Housing Scheme

In 1955, the British government introduced in Singapore, then a colony of the British empire, a social security scheme, called the Central Provident Fund scheme (CPF), with the objective of initiating saving for retirement. Under this scheme, both employees and employers were required to contribute five percent of the employee's salary to the employee's CPF account. The money would be kept by the CPF Board for safekeeping and CPF members are allowed to withdraw their savings from this Fund only at the age of 55 (for a complete discussion of the CPF scheme, see Chew and Chew, 2008). The People's Action Party (PAP) led by Mr Lee Kuan Yew won the General election in 1959 when Singapore was granted self-government. Mr Lee, the then-Prime Minister, immediately engineered a series of economic and social measures to attract foreign investment. The measures were so effective in drawing foreign investment into Singapore that by the late 1960s, Singapore faced a labor shortage.

In an attempt to prevent wages from rising too fast given the labor shortage, the economy adopted a deliberate policy to lure married women back into the labor force and to import foreign workers. At the same time, the government raised the CPF contribution rate for both employees and employers gradually. By 1971, the CPF contribution rate for both employees and employers was 10 percent. This meant an increase in labor costs. However, despite those measures the government was still fearful of runaway wages, which would have retarded the economy's industrial growth. Hence, the government set up the National Wages Council (NWC) to ensure that wages would rise in an orderly manner (for a complete discussion on the NWC, see Lim and Chew, 1998). With the inception of the NWC, which is tripartite in nature, in 1972, Singapore enjoyed high wage growth and CPF contribution rates were raised to 15.5 percent by 1977.

Singaporeans did not mind the higher CPF contribution rates because since the mid-1960s, the Singapore government had permitted Singaporeans to make use of their CPF balances to finance their housing mortgage. This conversion of the CPF from basically a retirement fund into a housing fund has enabled Singapore to achieve its high home ownership target. The high level of home ownership and the fact that rising property prices benefited the people of Singapore meant that the PAP government was riding high as it was able to fulfill the aspirations of Singaporeans. It is therefore not surprising that the PAP has won all the General Elections from 1959 (see Pugalenthi, 1996, for the election results in Singapore, and Tay and Yeo, 2006, for information on elections in Asia). Any backlash which could have arisen from the increase in employers' CPF contribution rate (which meant an increase in labor costs) did not come about because the economy was strong and the labor market tight in the late 1960s. (It should be noted, however, that the government was aware that the CPF was essentially meant as a retirement scheme in the first place. Hence, in 1977, the CPF account was split into two accounts: the Ordinary Account; which could be used for investments such as housing, and the Special Account which is specifically reserved for retirement.) By 1977, both the employees' and employers' contribution rate was 15.5 percent (Chew and Chew, 2008).

Using the CPF to Restructure the Manufacturing Sector

In 1978, China's leaders decided to adopt the capitalist policy to develop China, and its paramount leader, Deng Xiaoping, visited Singapore to learn about the market economy. The Singapore government then foresaw that the Chinese economy would become a formidable competitor in labor-intensive exports. Consequently, the government and the NWC attempted to encourage Singapore's industries to restructure from labor-intensive to capital-intensive production methods by raising employers' CPF contribution rate from 16.5 percent in 1978 sharply to 20.5 percent in 1979, and then more gradually to 22 percent in 1982. By 1984, employers' CPF contribution rate stood at 25 percent. (Employees' CPF contribution rates for 1978, 1979, 1982 and 1984 respectively were 16.5 percent, 16.5 percent, 23 percent and 25 percent.) The resultant increase in labor costs forced firms in Singapore to automate. Firms which could not cope with the rising labor costs migrated to Malaysia. The people of Singapore were very pleased. They enjoyed high wage growth and full employment; they had huge CPF savings which they used to finance their housing mortgages; they used some of their CPF balances to buy shares; and some even used part of their CPF balances to pay for the tertiary education of their children. The labor movement, which is represented by the National Trades Union Congress (NTUC), has been lauded as a reliable partner in the growth of the Singapore economy (see Chew and Chew, 1995, for more discussion on the role of the NTUC).

The Regional Recession in 1985

In late 1985, commodity prices fell to a level which adversely affected the Malaysian and Indonesian economies. Combined with the fact that Singapore's labor costs had risen significantly and given the strong Sing dollar, the regional recession caused Singapore's exports to suffer a decline. The resultant huge increase in unemployment was inevitable. This was a dire situation for Singapore because we have no unemployment benefits scheme, and the reach of social welfare schemes was not extensive as the

Singapore economy was based on strong economic fundamentals (see Lim and Associates, 1988, for a complete analysis of the Singapore economy during the 1985 recession).

The NWC met and diagnosed the situation. The consensus was that the Singapore economy was caught in the regional recession affecting Malaysia, Indonesia and Singapore, and that the high labor cost in Singapore must be brought down to make our exports more competitive so that there will be an increase in exports to the developed countries.

There are three mechanisms which can be used to reduce labor costs:

(i)   The devaluation mechanism, allowing the Sing dollar to fall in value. However, the devaluation mechanism can trigger off retaliation from our competitors, leading to a situation of competitive devaluation. At the same time, any devaluation would cause the inflation rate in Singapore to rise, which would offset any cost saving that can be gained from devaluation.

(ii) The foreign exchange reserves mechanism, using the nation's foreign exchange reserves to subsidize employers' CPF contributions. This would not cause hardship to Singaporeans. But the adoption of such a mechanism may foster a dependency mentality and lead to the habit of resorting to the use of our foreign exchange reserves whenever any emergency arises. Nurturing such a habit would result in rapid depletion of our national reserves.

(iii) The industrial relations mechanism, placing the burden of labor cost adjustments on our workers. This was the most difficult option as both the government and the unions knew that this was highly unpopular, and that activating this mechanism would cause hardship to many people and would get some Singaporeans into difficulty in financing their mortgage payments.

However, the general public was aware of only two possible mechanisms, the industrial relations mechanism and the devaluation mechanism. Using our national reserves to help fund the CPF contributions was unheard of at that time.

With the support of the government, the NWC decided to recommend a wage freeze and a reduction of the employers' CPF contribution rate from 25 percent to 10 percent in 1986. In total, Singapore workers gave up 15 percent of CPF savings and three to seven percent of foregone wage increases that year. No government has ever succeeded in ordering or even proposing a wage reduction of that magnitude on a nation-wide basis without suffering a backlash. How did Singapore achieve such a large wage reduction without strikes and without workers protesting on the streets?

The goodwill that existed among the government, the NTUC and the workers had been nurtured over the years through the NWC's principle of growth with equity. Every Singaporean family benefited during the good years. At the beginning of the 1985 recession, the government, the NTUC and the NWC made an effort to explain to Singaporeans that the quickest way to recover from the recession was to lower wage costs overnight. This was only possible through a mandatory reduction of the employers' CPF contribution rate. The government and the NWC had also promised that once the recession is over, the employers' contribution rate would be restored. For those who had mortgage payment problems due to the reduction of the employers' contribution rate, the government persuaded the banks to extend the period of their housing loans so that monthly mortgage installments would be smaller. This, indeed, was a socialist maneuver by the Singapore government, getting everyone to accept a cut in salary so that the nation could recover quickly from the recession. In this way, the political capital that the NWC had built up over the years was converted into an economic instrument which came in useful at the right time.

The reduction in labor cost which was aimed at through lowering the employers' CPF contribution rate was a calculated risk, one that would increase significantly if recovery did not occur soon enough. Fortunately, the Singapore economy recovered in 1987.

While the quick recovery was in part due to the lowering of the labor cost, more importantly it was because Singapore was able to export to the developed countries which had enjoyed good GDP growth.

As the Singapore economy recovered in 1987, the employers' CPF contribution was restored, as promised, to 12 percent in 1988 and to 15 percent in 1989. The PAP government won big again at the National Elections in 1988, showing that the Singapore society at large was supportive of the government policy of lowering the employers' CPF contribution rate.

The PAP government retained power again in the 1991 National Elections. The people of Singapore again enjoyed increases in the employers' CPF contribution rate, which was raised to 20 percent by 1994. While the employers' contribution rate had been increased, the employees' CPF contribution rate (which had remained at 25 percent through the recession) was lowered to 20 percent to match the employers' rate by 1994. This fall in the employees' CPF contribution rate had the effect of giving Singaporeans more take-home pay.

East Asian Currency Crisis, 1997, and SARS, 2003

As is well-known, the 1997 East Asian Currency crisis took the world by surprise. The Singapore dollar depreciated against the US dollar by about 20 percent, and the stock market and property indices fell by more than 50 percent (see Lim Chong Yah, 2007, for an analysis of the crisis). The unemployment rate rose again as a result of the Currency Crisis, and also because of the keen competition from China. During this crisis, Singaporeans were more prepared and knew that the impending reduction of the employers' CPF contribution rate was inevitable. Indeed, the employers' CPF contribution rate was reduced from 20 percent to 10 percent in 1999 for the purpose of protecting employment via a reduction in the labor cost.

Although Singapore's financial sector was badly damaged, the lowering of the labor cost helped Singapore's exports to USA and

Europe, which were not affected by the Asian Currency Crisis. Consequently, the Singapore economy recovered well in 1999–2000, and subsequently the employers' CPF contribution rate was raised to 12 percent in 2000, and again to 16 percent in 2003.

However, SARS hit a few Asian cities, including Singapore, in 2003. Being a city state, the Singapore economy was badly affected and its unemployment rate again rose. The Singapore government reluctantly reduced the employers' CPF contribution rate to 13 percent in 2004. As the Singapore economy recovered well during 2006–7, the employers' CPF contribution rate was again restored to 14.5 percent in 2007. It should be noted, however, that the impact of the employers' CPF contribution rate on labor cost was by then not as important as it once was. This is due to the fact that the CPF contributions are now capped at the monthly wage ceiling of $4,500 since 2006 (Chew and Chew, 2008).

New Way to Use Singapore's Political Capital

The Singapore economy performed rather poorly during 2002–2004 (Chew, 2006). SARS was a reason for the poor performance, but more importantly, Singapore might have priced itself out of the export market due to the higher cost of doing business in Singapore. Singapore needed new strategies to generate growth and prevent the unemployment rate from rising. Hence, the following strategies were adopted:

Firstly, Singapore decided to build the Integrated Resorts (IRs) which would have a casino as an important tourist attraction. The Singapore society at large was undecided over the issue of the casino. Many religious organizations openly disapproved of this decision. The government took pains to explain to Singaporeans that gambling is already widely accessible because of the various social and technological developments, and many Singaporeans do go on cruises in the open seas to gamble. Hence, it was argued that the impact of gambling on locals would be marginal. Furthermore, the government promised that more manpower would be added to the Ministry in charge of social welfare to facilitate the launching of moral programmes and the counseling of gambling addicts so that the negative impact would be minimized. In initiating the IRs project, the government was using its political capital, just as it did in reducing the employers' CPF contribution rate in 1986.

Secondly, knowing that the unemployment rate was on an upward trend, the government's informal policy of helping Singaporeans in financial need has been beefed up and improved upon (see Chew, 2006).

Thirdly, together with the NTUC, the government provided grants to encourage firms in Singapore to re-design their jobs to encourage local workers to take up such jobs instead of having firms rely on foreign workers.

Fourthly, the Singapore government launched an Income Supplement programme, under which low-wage native workers would receive a supplement of about eight percent of their wages annually, provided that these workers remain employed.

From 2005, Singapore' economic performance was quite healthy. In mid-2008, the unemployment rate in Singapore was 1.6 percent, and there were more than 750,000 foreign workers and about 150,000 professionals working in Singapore. The strategies adopted apparently have worked well.

Since early 2008, all countries had faced rising food and oil prices. Singapore was no exception. Having a strong reserves position, the Singapore government permitted the appreciation of the Sing dollar in an attempt to keep the inflation rate down. But the exchange rate policy this time around was not effective because, while the strong Sing dollar did not hurt Singapore's exports much in the US market as other currencies have also appreciated, Singapore imports food from other Asian countries, whose currencies have also appreciated against the US dollar (the only exception being the Indonesian Rupiah). Hence, despite a strong Sing dollar, Singapore's inflation rate was at an all-time high of 6 percent in 2008.

The Singapore government has used its political capital as an economic instrument both for stability and also for competitiveness. This strategy of the PAP government of using political capital has proven to be effective and productive. However, it is effective because it delivered each time. But that does not guarantee that this will always be the case.

2009 Global Financial Tsunami

Since September 2008, the economic fortune of the world has turned upside down. In the early part of 2008, we were worried about inflation. The unusually high food and oil prices in early 2008 had triggered a huge transfer of wealth from the households, firms and governments of oil-importing countries to the oil-exporting countries. (On hindsight, this transfer actually made oil-importing countries less able to cope with any financial crisis. Consequently, many individuals, firms, financial institutions, and governments in the oil-importing countries were threatened with an insolvency problem when there is any financial hiccup, let alone a financial tsunami of the current scale.)

But by the later part of 2008, the situation had completely reversed: we are now all concerned about deflation and recession. Stocks, properties and all sorts of financial products have fallen in value. Many banks and financial institutions face insolvency. It is not hard to see the problem. All business entities have a balance sheet. While the total liabilities have not diminished due to the financial crisis, the value of all assets including financial products has fallen drastically and some have become worthless. The balance sheets of all highly leveraged firms and individuals have been badly damaged. The banking sector has been also badly hit as many banks are struck with almost worthless financial products (toxic assets). Hence, the banks cannot or are reluctant to make loans, and this has exacerbated the already worsening economic condition. The volume of trade worldwide has fallen. The global financial tsunami started in the USA, and has spread to all the developed countries. The Asian countries also suffer because of the decline in exports and reduction in foreign direct investment. The episode is still unfolding. But the popular view is that the USA economy will not hit bottom until late 2009.

Singapore is in uncharted waters, as indeed is the whole world. During the 1985 recession, Singapore along with Malaysia and Indonesia registered negative GDP growth. But at that time the rest of the world was healthy. Hence we could lower our labor cost and were able to recover quickly as our exports increase. During the 1997 East Asian Crisis, Singapore was again badly affected; but again we could rely on lower labor cost to increase our exports to USA and Europe, and hence we also recovered quite quickly. But in this current financial crisis, no country is doing well. USA, Europe and Japan are all in recession. Oil-rich countries such as Russia also suffer because of lost oil revenue as the price of oil has fallen significantly. Export-led countries such as China and India, and almost all developing countries including Singapore suffer either in terms of an economic slowdown or a recession. The Singapore government predicts that the GDP of the Singapore economy will decline to a range of –5 percent to –2 percent for 2009 (Singapore Budget 2009). The NTUC expects the number of retrenchments to be around 30,000 for 2009. What measures can the government of Singapore adopt to help the economy recover?

As pointed out in the early part of this paper, there are three mechanisms by which labor cost can be reduced: the industrial relations mechanism, the devaluation mechanism and the foreign exchange reserves mechanism. However, one may question what can Singapore do to counter a global recession. We cannot export our way out of recession this time around. If we could lower our labor cost by devaluing the Sing dollar, can we reduce unemployment by exporting more? Who will buy our exports? If we adopt the industrial relations mechanism to help us reduce our labor cost by reducing employers' CPF contribution rate from the current 14.5 percent to, say 5 percent, the disposable income of Singapore workers would be very much reduced. Against a backdrop of reducing income or worse, losing jobs, many Singapore families would have difficulty meeting their monthly mortgage payments. A sub-prime crisis may take place in Singapore as a result, and that would wipe out any political capital that the Singapore government or the labor movement has. Many analysts therefore predict that the industrial relations mechanism would not be adopted this time.

None predicted that the foreign exchange reserves mechanism would ever be triggered off. But they were wrong.

Budget 2009

Singapore analysts expected that the Singapore Budget for 2009 would be extraordinary, and it was. Budget 2009 brought Singapore a resilience package of $20.5 billion for 2009. The main component is a jobs credit scheme, under which employers will receive a 12 percent cash grant on the first $2,500 of each month's wages for each employee on their CPF payroll for one year in the first instance. This scheme means that, for employers employing Singaporeans and permanent residents, their employers' CPF contribution rate would be reduced by nine percent. Unlike past reductions in labor cost, this reduction in labor cost will not be borne by our workers, but will be financed by our foreign exchange reserves. The government has made it very clear that the main purpose of the jobs credit scheme is to protect employment or to reduce retrenchment.

In addition to the jobs credit scheme, there will be an expanded version of the skills upgrading programme — the Skills Programme for Up-grading and Resilience (SPUR). SPUR will pay for 90 percent of the cost of training and 90 percent of absentee payrolls for workers who take part in the training programme. This means that, under this scheme, firms in Singapore will pay only 10 percent of their workers' wages if they send their workers for training.

As part of the social safety net, the government also will give low-income workers a temporary wage payment under the Workfare Income Supplement (WIS). WIS is critical as we expect wages to fall during 2009.

Can the Old Mechanism Work?

We still rely on the CPF scheme to reduce labor cost. We did that in 1986, in 1999 and 2003. And we are doing it again in 2009.

Would it have the same impact? We refrained from using the foreign exchange reserves mechanism in the earlier crises in our attempts to reduce the labor cost. On hindsight, the industrial relations mechanism was correct. Recovery was fast. This time around, we do not expect exports to rise due to jobs credit scheme and SPUR, because the malaise is global. What Budget 2009 does is to buy us some time to wait out the global recession. If 2010 comes with practically the same bad news, the jobs credit scheme and SPUR will have to continue for one more year while we continue to wait for the global economy to recover. However, we do not wait in idleness. We train our workers while we wait for the global recession to pass over. Our strategy of not using the foreign exchange reserves mechanism in the past was correct because our use of the industrial relations mechanism was to reduce labor cost was enough to enable us to increase our exports. This kept our foreign exchange reserves intact, and this is why we still have formidable foreign exchange reserves to fall back on, and this is the main reason why the Singapore dollar does not collapse. If the Sing dollar were to collapse, we would be like Iceland. The standard of living of Singaporeans would have plunged.

Conclusion

In many countries, both developed and developing, the ability of workers to cope with recession is based on unemployment benefits schemes or handouts. This results in huge budget deficits to current account deficits and a weak national currency in the long term. Singapore took the harder approach by encouraging workers to be self-reliant. As a result, we were able to use the industrial relations mechanism to reduce labor costs. The use of this mechanism has enabled Singapore to minimize spending on unnecessary social welfare, which most countries have not been able to achieve.

The Singapore story is one that shows that as individuals and as a nation, we have accumulated reserves through our personal savings and in foreign exchange reserves during periods of prosperity as well as of normalcy. Our CPF scheme has saved many Singaporeans from losing sleep in the current financial crisis. And we can count on our foreign exchange reserves to buy us time to recover from the current global crisis. This is a precious gift from our collective wisdom that some countries do not have.

References

Chew, S. B. and R. Chew (2008). Macro Objectives of the CPF Scheme. In *Singapore and Asia in a Globalized World: Contemporary Economic Issues and Policies*. Singapore: World Scientific.

Chew. S. B. (2006). Resilience of the Singapore Economy and the Adequacy of the Social Security System. In *Singapore Perspectives 2006, Going Global: Being Singaporean in a Globalised World*. Institute of Policy Studies, Singapore: Marshall Cavendish Academic.

Chew, S. B. and R. Chew (1995). *Employment-Driven Industrial Relations Regimes: The Singapore Experience*. UK: Avebury.

Lim, C. Y. (2007). Ten years after the meltdown in Asia: Are our economies more vulnerable or robust. Key note speech at Asian Business Case Competition at NTU, 9 October, 2007.

Lim, C. Y. and Associates. (1988). *Policy Options for the Singapore Economy*. Singapore: McGrawHill.

Lim C. Y. and R. Chew (1998). *Wages and Wages Policies Tripartism in Singapore*. Singapore: World Scientific.

Pugalenthi Sr. (1996). *Elections in Singapore*. VJ Times.

Singapore Budget 2009, http://www.singaporebudget.gov.sg/speech_pa/pa.html#s1.

Tay, S. and L. H. Yeo (2006). *Elections In Asia: Making Democracy Work?* Singapore: Marshall Cavendish International.

CHAPTER 5

The On-going Global Financial Crisis and Asian Regionalism

PRADUMNA B. RANA

The Asian financial crisis of 1997–1998 marks a watershed in Asian economic development because, in the post-crisis period, Asian countries started to support market-led integration with various policy efforts. This paper argues that the on-going global financial crisis of 2008 has strengthened the case for Asian regionalism further and outlines a set of policy actions which could be considered at the regional (Asia-wide) level to complement those being implemented by individual countries. Coordinated regional responses are expected to be more effective than unilateral ones.

I. Introduction

Despite the lack of an integrationist approach in the East Asian development model, for various reasons, since the financial crisis of 1997–1998, East Asia has embarked on and made commendable progress in supporting market-led integration with various policy efforts (ADB, 2008; Rana, 2009a; Kawai and Rana, 2009). These include, among others, the ASEAN+3 Economic Review and Policy Dialogue (ERPD), the Chiang Mai Initiative (CMI), and the

81

ASEAN+3 Asian Bond Market Initiative. Economic linkages between East Asia and South Asia are also surging — albeit from low bases — paving the way for an eventual integrated Pan-Asia (Rana, 2008; Rana, 2009b; and Francois, Rana, and Wignaraja, 2009). Various new sub-regional/regional groupings such as the BIMSTEC, ASEAN+3, and the East Asia Summit have also been established.

The paper has two objectives: (i) to argue that the on-going global financial crisis (GFC) has further strengthened the case for Asian regionalism and (ii) to outline a set of policies that Asian countries could consider at the regional level to support actions being taken by individual countries.

Section II of the paper reviews the causes of the subprime mortgage crisis (SMC) in the US and the GFC, and Section III outlines the impacts of these crises on Asian countries. Section IV summarizes the actions taken at the individual country level, while Section V highlights the case for strengthening Asian regionalism: it also outlines actions that Asian countries could consider at the regional level. Actions are also being taken to reform the international financial architecture, but these are not discussed in the paper.

II. Causes of the SMC and the GFC

The proximate cause or the trigger of the SMC was the bursting of the housing bubble in the US during the summer of 2007 when subprime defaults began to rise and foreclosures increased. It then spread to prime loans and other types of consumer credit. Various types of financial institutions, particularly those with large exposures to subprime-related structured products, became affected leading to a series of failures of several large financial institutions (e.g., Bear Stearns, American Insurance Group, and Lehman Brothers).

The root causes of the SMC were, however, policy mistakes in the US, the global imbalances, and the weaknesses in the regulation and supervision of the financial sector in the country.

A number of policy mistakes were made during the past three decades. First, after the bursting of the dot.com bubble in

1999–2000, the US Fed ran a loose monetary policy for several years. The Federal Funds rate dropped from 5.98 percent in January 2001 to 1.73 percent two years later and stayed at about that level until 2005. This fueled a credit boom in the US. Second, the repeal of the Glass–Steagall Act in 1999 during the Clinton Administration opened the gates for US non-banks to take on the full range of risky assets (securities, derivatives, and structured products) either directly on the balance sheets or indirectly through off-balance sheet conduits. This worked well in Germany and the other European countries, but not in the US where investment banks were generally outside the preview of regulators. So commercial banks and investment banks went into complex derivative securities and also extensively leveraged their operations. The existing regulatory system was too weak to cover investment banks.

The large and growing global imbalances — the current account deficits in the US which reached the critical level of five percent of GDP or more over the past five years and surpluses in Asia — and the recycling of Asia surpluses through purchase of US Treasuries, further fuelled the credit boom in the US. It is interesting to note that the often repeated warnings that the global imbalance could lead to a disorderly adjustment of the dollar (for example, made by the IMF staff) did not materialize. The credit boom made possible by the imbalance led, however, to a build-up of vulnerability in the US by fuelling the housing boom and extension of credit to subprime lenders (people who did not meet credit quality requirements).

The weak regulatory and supervisory systems in the US were also at fault. Banks and savings and loans provided money to home buyers through mortgage loans. In the bygone era, these financial institutions would have held on and collected interest and repayments. In the modern era, housing finance institutions repackaged mortgage loans into bundles of mortgage-backed securities (MBSs) with "triple A" ratings from credit rating agencies and sold them. Financial institutions did not hold on in this originate-and-distribute model. MBSs were further sliced and diced into derivative assets through the process of financial engineering and sold to investors all over the world. Major chunks of these assets were moved to the books of separate structured investment vehicles in order to make balance sheets of financial institutions look healthier than they actually were. Credit default swaps provided by large insurers such as the American Insurance Group were used to insure these assets against default risks. There was also excessive leveraging and irresponsible lending. Allen Greenspan, the Chief of the Federal Reserve System for 18 years of this boom period, confessed that he had faith that financial institutions were prudent enough to make sure that they were not lending money cheaply to people who could not pay it back. But this is exactly what happened. Self-regulation did not work. Incentive compensation of CEOs of financial institutions was also very high. Much of this was possible because of the decision by the Securities and Exchange Commission in 2004 to permit these types of activities. The SEC also dismantled its supervisory unit during that year.

The SMC spread around the world especially after September/ October 2008, as banks holding toxic assets engineered in the US faced difficulties. In addition to this direct effect, there were the indirect effects due to the capital flows and the trade channels. Before the outbreak of the SMC, many emerging markets were receiving abundant amounts of private capital and discussions focused on the possibility of such inflows undermining the macroeconomic and financial sector stability. Since then, such inflows dried up leading to huge asset price depreciations and collapse in demand. Capital was sucked back into the developed countries to restore damaged balance sheets, meet margin calls, and accommodate large withdrawals. According to the IIF, inflows into emerging markets which were $929 billion in 2007 are expected to fall to $165 billion in 2009.

The synchronized slowdown in the industrialized countries also had a negative impact on real economic activity of emerging markets through the trade channel as import demand in the industrial world collapsed. The SMC, therefore, became a GFC.

Summing up, aside from the global imbalance problem where the responsibility is shared between the US and the rest of the world, the SMC and the GFC are "crisis made in and exported by the US". This is unlike previous crises which originated mainly in the emerging markets.

Similarities Between the SMC/GFC, the Asian Financial Crisis (AFC), and the Latin American Crisis

No two financial crises are the same. Hence there are similarities as well as differences between the SMC/GFC, the AFC, and the Latin American debt crisis of the mid-1980s (Table 5.1).

As noted in a recent article by Reinhart and Reinhart (2008), all episodes of "capital flow bonanza" ultimately lead to a financial crash. In this vein, all three crises under discussion were associated with sharp surges in inflow and outflow of foreign capital. In the Latin American and the SMC/GFC cases, it was the governments that borrowed large amounts of capital from abroad to finance their monetary and fiscal profligacy, whereas in the case of the AFC, it

Table 5.1: Similarities and differences between the SMC/GFC, AFC, and the Latin American Crisis.

Causes	SMC/GFC	AFC	Latin American Crisis
Proximate/ Trigger	Bursting of the housing bubble	Large withdrawal of capital by private investors	Large capital outflow to service debt
Root Causes	– Policy mistakes	– Premature capital account liberalization	– Large and growing fiscal and current account deficits
	– Global payments imbalance and liquidity	– Pegged exchange rates	
	– Weak regulation and supervision of financial sector	– Weak regulation and supervision of financial sector and corporates	

was the private financial sector and corporates that borrowed in international markets. A lot more institutions were involved in the latter case making it more complicated to manage. While there were sharp withdrawals of capital from Latin America and Asia during the crisis, capital inflows into the US have been fairly resilient, reflecting the international reserve asset and safe haven role of the US dollar. Weak regulatory and supervisory frameworks of banks were an important root cause of the SMC/GFC and the AFC but not in the case of the Latin American debt crisis.

While the Latin American debt crisis was a current account crisis, the AFC was a capital account crisis associated with investor panic, a sharp withdrawal of foreign capital, and liquidity crunch. The SMC/GFC is a mixture of the two — associated with large inflows of financial capital to finance growing fiscal and current account deficits.

III. The Impact of the SMC/GFC on Asia

The Asian countries were relatively unscathed by the SMC during the early stage of the crisis. This was because Asian banks were less exposed to the toxic assets that were engineered and crafted in the US. According to data from various issues of the *Economist* and *Financial Times*, of the $500 billion written off by banks globally in the year to August 2008, Asian financial institutions (including those in Japan) accounted for only five percent. Also Asian financial sectors were relatively resilient — thanks to the reforms implemented during and after the Asian Financial Crisis (AFC) of 1997–1998. For example, the average capital-adequacy ratio for Asian banks stands at a healthy 12 percent and Tier-1 capital ratio which was around five percent in Indonesia and Malaysia in 1997 has increased to 10 percent. Since the AFC, significant progress has been made in improving risk management systems, regulatory and supervisory systems, and corporate governance. Within the region, vulnerability is the highest in the case of Australia and Korea as they have high loan/deposit ratios — 125 percent as compared to the Asian average of 90 percent.

But after September/October 2008, the indirect effects of the GFC have affected the Asian countries very strongly as they are among the most open in the world. Foreign capital inflows slowed considerably as commercial banks, foreign institutional investors and others withdrew funds to meet redemptions back home. According to the latest IIF data, private capital flows to emerging Asia declined from $516.7 billion to 2007 to an estimated $134.4 billion in 2008. Bank lending declined the most followed by equity both direct and indirect. In 2009, these flows are projected to be only $44.1 billion. Since the beginning of 2008, stock markets (in US dollar terms) have tumbled by about 62 percent in Indonesia and India, followed by Singapore, Thailand and Taiwan where they fell by about 50 percent, and in Malaysia by about 40 percent. The Chinese stock markets have been the worst performer in the region falling by over 65 percent. Asian stock markets have fallen more than, say, the Dow Jones index which fell by 31 percent. Asian currencies have also taken a beating. Remittances have also started to slow in the top-three recipients in Asia — China, India, and the Philippines.

In addition to the "capital flows" channel, the "trade channel" demand for Asian exports has also slowed dramatically because of the synchronized global slowdown. Singapore and Hong Kong, which are very open economies, are already in a recession. The Chinese and the Indian economies have slowed considerably.

Growth forecasts for Asia from both private as well as public sources (including the ADB, IMF, and the World Bank) have been marked down considerably. For example, in February, the IMF slashed its growth forecast for the region to 2.7 percent on average from 4.9 percent only two months ago. The IMF issued a worrying prognosis for Korea predicting that its economy could contract by four percent this year. The forecasts for the Chinese economy also have been marked down and the social impacts of the crisis including unrests are being felt as millions join the ranks of the unemployed. Consensus Economics has also slashed its 2009 growth forecasts for Asian countries. For China, from 9.3 percent in July 2008 to 7.4 percent in January 2009. The corresponding figures are 4.7 percent and 0.6 percent for Korea and 8 percent and 5.6 percent for India.

IV. Individual Country Responses

In an attempt to promote greater financial stability in the context of the GFC, several Asian countries have announced full deposit insurance guarantees for a number of years (Hong Kong, Taiwan, Australia, and Singapore). Also in an attempt to rebalance economic growth, many Asian countries have announced consecutive cuts in interest rates (for example, China has cut interest rates five times since September and twice lowered the reserve requirement) and fiscal stimulus packages (China, India, Japan, Australia, Korea, and Malaysia). In January, Singapore announced an expansionary pro-business package amounting to six percent of its GDP. Altogether, Asian countries have pledged more than $685 for stimulus. Among the stimulus packages, China's two-year $600 billion package accounting for 16 percent of its GDP is the biggest, bigger than the US package of $860 billion which accounts for five percent of its GDP. One-half of this amount is to be spent on infrastructure development including airport, highways and railways and the rest on social welfare, environment, and technological innovation. Although it is uncertain how much of this is new money and how much already in the pipeline, the stimulus package seeks to maintain the growth rate at over the psychological mark of eight percent.

In Asia, so far, there has been no need to either recapitalize banks or to bail them out by removing toxic assets. These cannot, however, be ruled out in the future as clouds darken on the horizon. If so, Asian countries should use their massive reserves that has been accumulated over the past decade — at a high cost, for they were invested mostly in low-yielding treasuries — to inject liquidity in their countries. This could be done by auctioning foreign exchange reserves. China holds about $2 billion of reserves, India another $250 billion, and Asia as a group (including Japan) holds two-thirds of the world's reserves. So far, it is only Singapore that has decided to use reserves to finance a temporary job credit program to subsidize part of the wage bill for employers and special risk-sharing initiatives to encourage banks to lend more freely to viable businesses.

V. The Case for Asian Regionalism and Possible Regional Actions

As noted in the previous section, most of the actions taken by the Asian countries, so far, have been at the individual country level. In addition, actions at the regional level are also urgently required. First, since 2000, regionalism has been an important component of Asia's trade strategy. The GFC, by providing opportunities for bold reforms to enhance competitiveness, should enable countries to find economies of scale at the regional level. Second, the GFC and the high and growing level of economic interdependence among Asian countries have increased the need for policy coordination at the regional level to take account of the spillover effects. Intra-regional trade among the ASEAN+3 is about 55 percent of its total trade because of the vertical division of labor through the establishment of regional production networks centered on China. Trade between ASEAN+3 and India (and other South Asian countries) is also surging (Rana, 2009b; and Francois, Rana, and Wignaraja, 2009). The level of financial integration among ASEAN+3, although low, is also starting to increase. There are, therefore, significant spillovers of policies which makes a strong case for coordinated policy actions among the Asian countries. Regional policy coordination could add value in, at least, two ways. First, policymakers tend to be more frank when discussing policies with neighboring countries than say at the global level. Second, the regional policy agenda also tend to be more focused on the common issues affecting a set of countries rather than those at global fora. Policy coordination does not mean identical policies, but broadly consistent policies at the regional level. Policy coordination will reduce the incidence of beggar-thy-neighbor type policies.

Third, the GFC has highlighted the urgent need for joint policy statements and show of force to reverse the flight of quality and loss of investor confidence in the region. Asian countries should work closely together and announce joint actions on policies to promote economic growth and financial stability such as expansionary monetary, fiscal, and financial sector measures. This will go a long way in reducing the crisis of confidence which is leading to overshooting with damages being much higher than those dictated by economic fundamentals. A coordinated response from Asia will be much more effective than unilateral actions.

Fourth, the GFC has once again revived interest in the reform of the international financial architecture and it appears that the G20 will be given the lead role in spearheading discussions on these issues. Asian countries should, therefore, coordinate their views and positions and make effective representation and make their voices heard at the G20.

What are the actions that Asian countries could take at the regional level?

(1) *Expand the Membership of ASEAN+3 to Include India and Eventually Establish an Integrated Pan-Asia*

Although ASEAN is central to Asian regionalism, the ASEAN+3 which also includes China, Korea, and Japan is more appropriate to represent the region in various international negotiations. Also given (i) the strengthening economic linkages of the ASEAN+3 with South Asia, particularly with India, and India's emergence in the world economy (Rana, 2009b), and (ii) following the East Asia Summit, Asia–Europe Finance Ministers meeting, and the Comprehensive Economic Partnership for East Asia models, ASEAN+3 should invite India to be a member of and contribute to its various initiatives. An expanded ASEAN+3 which includes India will have a greater clout globally and be more legitimate regionally. The remaining members of the East Asia Summit (Australia and New Zealand) could also be brought in if there is a consensus among countries.

(2) *Strengthen the ASEAN+3 Economic Review and Policy Dialogue (ERPD)*

Although policy coordination could be conducted informally, support of an institutional arrangement where policymakers could meet and hold discussions among each other could be useful. Such an institutional arrangement in Asia could be an expanded ASEAN+3 Economic Review and Policy Dialogue (ERPD) process which includes India. Under the present process, Finance Ministers of the ASEAN+3 countries meet once a year and their Deputies twice a year for two days a time to (i) assess global, regional, and national conditions and risks (ii) review financial sector (including bond markets) development and vulnerabilities, and (iii) other topics of interest. This process should be strengthened to (i) move the dialogues which are in the "information sharing" stage to a "peer review" mechanism similar to that of the OECD Working Party 3 and eventually to a "due diligence" stage if a centralized reserve pool, independent of the IMF, were to be established in the region (ii) include central banks governors in the meeting of Finance Ministers and (iii) monitor the region's financial markets and their vulnerabilities (Kawai and Rana, 2008). A professional secretariat should also be established to support the ERPD/CMI process.

(3) *Establish an Asian Financial Stability Dialogue (AFSD)*

A recent ADB study (ADB, 2008) has proposed the establishment of the Asian Financial Stability Dialogue — an Asian version of the Financial Stability Forum — to bring together all responsibilities (including finance ministries, central bank authorities, and other financial regulators and supervisors) to address financial market vulnerabilities, regulations, and efforts at integration, as well as to engage in dialogue with the private sector. An expanded ASEAN+3 could help build a consensus on establishing the Asian Financial Stability Dialogue.

The immediate task of the AFSF would be to consider appropriate responses to the GFC and to address the regulatory and supervisory issues arising out of the GFC. Subsequently, the AFSD could develop and modify various financial sector codes and standards, foster the growth of regional bond markets, and assess the region's future vulnerability to a crisis by using an early warning system (ESW). Much work in this regard has already been done by the ASEAN+3 together with the ADB (ADB, 2007; Zhuang and

Rana, 2005). First, the currency and banking crisis EWS have been developed which use 40 leading indicators that have good predictive powers for historical crisis events. These leading indicators monitor current and capital account positions, monetary and fiscal conditions, real sector performance, capital markets, and global economic and financial conditions. The composite leading indexes constructed from the 40 leading indicators provide aggregate measures of macroeconomic vulnerability. On the basis of these aggregate measures, one can assign a specific period a particular alert level, indicating the state of a country's vulnerability to a currency or systemic banking crisis in that period. A software program has been developed to detect vulnerabilities. Second, the ASEAN+3 and the ADB have also developed a system to assess the financial health of banks, non-bank financial institutions, and capital markets by identifying a set of financial soundness indicators (formerly, aggregated micro-prudential indicators) that cover capital adequacy, asset quality, management efficiency, earnings and profitability, liquidity, and sensitivity to market risks (or CAMELS-type indicators). These are supplemented by capital market indicators and indicators of structural weaknesses. Third, a secure sub-site has been developed so that countries can exchange and share confidential data and EWS results among each other. Fourth, a Technical Working Group on Economic and Financial Monitoring has also been established to support the dialogues. These activities and systems, however, need to be strengthened further, implemented more effectively, and the results deliberated in appropriate fora in an attempt to prevent financial crises in the future.

(4) *Establish the Self-managed Reserve Pool*

The on-going efforts to establish a self-managed reserve pool by multilateralizing the bilateral swaps under the ASEAN+3 Chiang Mai Initiative should be expedited. Last May, the ASEAN+3 Finance Ministers had, in principle, agreed to establish a $80 billion pool and the details are to be agreed on by May 2009. The GFC has made the establishment of the ASEAN+3 self-managed reserve pool, augmenting its resources (say, doubling), and delinking it from IMF programs more urgent as roughly one-half of the resources of IMF of $250 billion has either been committed or is close to being committed to countries like Iceland, Ukraine, Hungary, Belarus, Pakistan, and other European countries that are lined up. Hence Asia should use its massive reserves to shield itself from the GFC. ASEAN+3 could help expedite the establishment of a self-managed reserve pooling the region and strengthening the ERPD to support it.

(5) *Establish an Asian Infrastructure Investment Fund and a Pan-Asian Infrastructure Forum*

As Kawai (2008) has suggested, Asian countries should also jointly boost fiscal spending by pooling reserves and establishing an infra-structure investment fund together with the ADB and accelerate spending on the various planned projects for high-quality infra-structure development (both physical and social). Expanded ASEAN+3 could help. This is a useful suggestion as infrastructure bottlenecks pose a major constraint in many countries in the region. The crisis could, therefore, provide an opportunity to alle-viate infrastructural constraints and barriers. Proposals to establish an Asian Infrastructure Fund and a Pan-Asian Investment Forum (ADBI 2009) should be considered.

(6) *China Could Consider Lending to the IMF If It Gets a Higher Quota*

Given the limited resources available at the IMF, there are on-going efforts to get China to lend a part of its reserves to the IMF. Japan recently agreed to lend $100 billion to the IMF. So far, China's response has been lukewarm and China has taken the position that the best action that it can take to support the global economy is to keep its own economy growing strongly. Any such lending by China should be conditional on raising the quota of China and India and the other emerging markets at the IMF. Presently, China's quota at the IMF is 3.7 percent and Germany's is six percent although

China has overtaken the latter country to become the third largest economy in the world. The US quota is 17 percent. Europe, as a group, holds about 39 percent and Japan six percent. Asian countries together have 25 percent.

(7) *Expanded ASEAN+3 Should Coordinate and Play an Active Role in the G20.*

Asian representatives at the G20 (Japan, China, Korea, India and Indonesia) should present Asian views and perspectives at these meetings. Expanded ASEAN+3 could help in developing a consensus on these matters. While the previous Managing Director of the IMF had placed a high priority on the reform of IMF quota to make the IMF a more legitimate global institution, actions on quota reforms appear to have subsided under the present Managing Director. The membership of the Financial Stability Forum should also be expanded in a similar fashion.

References

ADB (2007). TA for Enhancing the Capacity of Selected ASEAN+3 Countries for Assessing Financial Vulnerabilities.

ADB (2008). *Emerging Asian Regionalism: A Partnership for Shared Prsoperity*. Manila.

ADB Institute (2009). *Infrastructure for a Seamless Asia*. Tokyo.

Francois, J., P. B. Rana and G. Wignaraja (2009). *Pan-Asian Integration: Linking East and South Asia*. Palgrave Macmillan.

Kawai, M. (2008). *Global Financial Crisis and Implications for ASEAN*. Singapore: Institute of Southeast Asian Studies.

Kawai, M. and P. B. Rana (2009). The Asian Financial Crisis Revisited: Lessons, Responses, and New Challenges. In Richard Carney (ed.), *Lessons from the Asian Financial Crisis*. New York: Rutledge, pp. 155–197.

Rana, P. B. (2008). Linking South Asia with East Asia: Trends, Potential, and Policies. Economic Growth Center Working Paper 2008/14, Singapore: Nanyang Technological University.

Rana, P. B. (2009a). Asian Economic Integration: The Role of Singapore. In Chia Wai Mun and Sng Hui Ying (eds.), *Singapore in Asia and in a Globalized World*. Singapore: World Scientific, pp. 121–140.

Rana, P. B. (2009b). *South Asia: Rising to the Challenge of Globalization*. Singapore: World Scientific.

Reinhart, C. M. and V. R. Reinhart (2008). Capital Flows Bonanza: An Encompassing View of the Past and Present. NBER Working Paper 14321.

Zhuang, J. and P. B. Rana (ed.) (2005). *Early Warning Systems for Financial Crises: Applications to East Asia*. London: Palgrave McMillan.

CHAPTER 6

Global Economic Crisis and Energy Security: Integrated Energy Market

YOUNGHO CHANG

An integrated energy market has been considered in the region as a strategy to achieve ensuring sufficient energy supply at affordable prices. This chapter reviews how existing integrated energy markets have been created and what kind of benefits they have brought. Upon these observations, it envisions how an integrated energy market in the region, as a way of coping with economic crises and achieving energy security, could be launched, and examines what has been done towards launching an integrated energy market, and suggests a short-term and long-term strategy to create such an integrated energy market in the region.

Introduction

Economic crises would pose a threat on economies through various channels such as drying up of and delaying investments, lower levels of capital accumulation, high rates of unemployment and lower economic growth. However, economic crises would provide opportunities of identifying the weaknesses of an economy that would in turn give the directions of reforming the structure of economies. Economic cooperation in a region or the world as a whole has emerged as one way of coping with the economic crises and strengthening the structure of an economy, and concerted efforts through economic cooperation have produced tangible positive outcomes and been proved as effective and operational for containing economic crises. The European Coalition for Coal and Steel in the 1950s, which later became a full-fledged economic, legal, monetary and political community, is a good example for such successful economic cooperation that was formed during economic hard times. The International Energy Agency (IEA) that was formed after the first oil shock in the late 1970s is another example of such workable cooperation to contain global economic problems through cooperation efforts.

The success of such economic cooperation is mainly hinged on the economic theory of comparative advantage, which states that when two individuals exchange their goods and services, both will benefit from trading. This is not only the case in a two-person exchange economy, but would be the case in a multiple-persons setting.[1] When two economies exchange their goods and services, they have a larger market compared to each economy alone. And mutually agreed rules and regulations in the enlarged market would bring more competition so that fair competition in the market would enhance the economic efficiency in the market.

Over the last several decades, integration has appeared in various areas such as international relations and trade. There are numerous examples of such integration: the United Nations for international relations, General Agreements on Tariffs and Trade (GATT) and World Trade Organization (WTO) for global trade. A free trade agreement (FTA) between two countries is a mutually exclusive integration for trading goods and services. Slightly different but built on the same concept of integration are the International Energy Agency (IEA), which has been formed by

---

[1] This is a well-known economic theorem of comparative advantage, which is first suggested by an English economist, David Ricardo (1772–1823).

developed nations after two oil shock in the 1970s.[2] The IEA is an outcome of such integration efforts especially for energy among energy-importing countries. However, under the IEA, the consolidated efforts do not necessarily mean an integrated energy market across member countries. Rather, a closer example for an integrated regional energy market is found in the prototype of the European Union that first appeared in 1951 as an agreement for coal and steel for European countries.

The underlying theme of forming such integration efforts in world economics and international relations represents our belief that cooperation is an effective way of containing economic crises by making the involved parties better-off rather than isolated efforts by an individual or country. This belief, then, leads us to the discussion of control and confinement versus cooperation and coordination in energy issues relating to the global economic crises. Do we prefer one over another or do we sustain an equal importance between the two? This chapter explores the prospects of an integrated energy market in the region as a means of overcoming economic crises and ensuring energy security, examines what it would bring to the region, and envisions how we could prepare to make such an integrated energy market full-fledged and well-functioning.

More specifically, it discusses why we need an integrated energy market (along with the definitions, scope and characteristics of the market) and what kind of gains we get from such an integrated energy market — economic, environmental, security, etc. These discussions are hinged mainly on the premise that we expect such an integrated energy market to improve the welfare of people in the region. It also reviews what we could learn from efforts of launching an integrated energy market in other regions such as EU in terms of (but not restricted to) setting goals, objectives and timelines of launching an integrated energy market (and common energy policy).

Following these discussions and reviews, this chapter examines what kind of efforts ASEAN or countries in the region have

---

[2] At the opposite side of the IEA is the Organization of the Petroleum Exporting Countries (OPEC), which is considered a dual of the IEA.

taken to launch an integrated energy market. It also questions
whether any organization has been set up to take a role in launching
an integrated energy market (or are there similar entities in the region
that do such a role currently). Specifically, it questions whether a few
coordinated efforts in the region such as the ASEAN Power Grid, the
Trans-ASEAN Pipeline or any other economic and energy cooperation and developments in the region like the Greater Mekong
Sub-region can be considered a necessary initial step for launching an
integrated energy market. As a way of constructing an integrated
regional energy market, this chapter suggests the region adopt a
"cooperative competition" framework. In the "cooperative competition" framework, the region works collectively towards increasing
the size of an economic pie or a market while each country competes
to catch a larger share of the pie in the integrated market.

Lessons Learned from Integrated Energy Markets

The European Union (EU) has shown that a full-fledged integrated
regional market from economic to political context can work well
and more importantly, has been successfully performing.[3] Its gross
domestic product (GDP) at purchasing power parity is estimated
US$14.43 trillion while US$16.62 trillion at the official exchange rate
in 2007 (this is larger than GDP of the world's largest economy as
an individual economy — the United States of America and covers
more than one third of world GDP). Its GDP growth rate is estimated three percent in 2007 and per capita GDP at purchasing power
parity is US$32,700 in 2007 (this is within the 30 highest coun-
tries).[4] The EU experiences provide a few lessons and point to the

---

[3] Jorgen Orstrom Moller presents a comprehensive analysis on European integration from basic principles, institutions, grand designs and the mechanics, among
others, in his book, *European Integration: Sharing Experiences*. Institute of Southeast
Asian Studies, Singapore, 2008.
[4] CIA the World Factbook — European Union (https://www.cia.gov/library/
publications/the-world-factbook/geos/ee.html#Econ) and *Pocket World in
Figures* 2008 *Edition*, *The Economist*, London, UK.

directions for initiating and constructing an integrated regional energy market. This section reviews the lessons learned from the EU experiences, examines the benefits from an integrated energy market and identifies possible obstacles and the status of implementing such an integrated regional energy market.

First, what do we learn from the efforts put into launching and sustaining an integrated market in the European Union? In a recent special report on the European Union, *The Economist* claims that "the European Union has been far more successful than anyone expected when the Treaty of Rome was signed half a century ago" though it faces a few big problems it needs to solve.[5] The European Union started and developed from a regional coalition for coal and steel set up in 1951. The European Economic Community (EEC) was officially established from the Treaty of Rome signed by six European countries (France, then West Germany, Italy, Belgium, the Netherlands and Luxemburg) in 1957 and it became a common market soon after. There were two events that had stimulated the formation of the EEC — the French National Assembly's rejection of the proposed European Defence Community in 1954 and the Suez Crisis in 1956. The former reasserted the importance of a nation-state in the Europe while the latter emphasized the urgency of a European community. With a successful implementation of a common currency for the EU since 1999, it now introduces more integrated markets into the community from electricity to energy and carbon rights. An integrated electricity pool between Nord Pool and Danish and Dutch electricity markets can shed some light on the way in which an integrated electricity market in the region should head. The common electricity market throughout the EU also gives valuable lessons for the region to germinate the idea of launching an integrated energy market. Establishing a so-called independent regulatory body is a pre-requisite for a successful integration of electricity markets while controlling market power is another critical factor to contain a successful integration and implementation of electricity market (Larsen *et al.*, 2006; Domanico, 2007; Lise, *et al.*, 2008).

---

[5] Fit at 50? A special report on the European Union (17 March 2007). *The Economist.*

Second, what kinds of benefits are possible from launching an integrated energy (or electricity) market in the region? A study that examines strategies for regionally integrating electricity supply in West Africa suggests an integrated approach in which fast retirement of the obsolete power plants are advised and new investment projects at the whole sub-regional level are coordinated (Gnansounou *et al.*, 2007).[6] This approach is compared with an "autarkical" strategy in which adequate expansion of national power generation systems is a standalone decision and the exchanges of electricity among the countries in sub-zones are considered and made. With simulations of a 'bottom-up" electricity system expansion planning optimization model, the study finds that an integrated strategy would bring benefits such as reduced capital expenditures, lower electricity supply cost, and the enhanced system reliability. Similarly the ASEAN Power Grid that connects the Indonesian archipelago, Singapore, Peninsular Malaysia, Kalimantan, the Philippines and the Greater Mekong sub-region would bring some benefits to the region. But the expected benefits that would be realized under such an integrated electricity grid (possibly together with a market) remain to be seen.

Third, have we implemented an initial step to build an integrated energy market in the region? What is necessary and appropriate for an integrated energy market? Is providing a portal for energy trading sufficient enough for launching such a market? If oil is the concern of the region for an integrated energy market, what can we provide to launch an integrated energy market for oil? Is setting up an oil trading floor enough to make such a market function properly? Could building an oil stockpile help in making the market function smoothly? Is a common oil stockpile necessary for a well-functioning integrated energy market? An oil stockpile in the region could supplement a common energy market by providing a buffer for a short-term fluctuation in oil supply or supply

---

[6] The countries in the region are Benin, Burkina Faso, Cape Verde, Ivory Coast, Gambia, Ghana, Guinea-Bissau, Liberia, Mali, Niger, Nigeria, Senegal, Sierra Leone, and Togo.

shortage, but its real effects on the market would be minimal as other oil stockpiles or the Strategic Petroleum Reserve of the US has shown. These appeared to have a relatively small impact on buffering highly volatile oil prices.

How could an integrated energy market in the region start? It can start from forming a common market for energy resources that are abundant and necessary in the region. The resources that fit with these characteristics are electricity and natural gas. This region has a huge potential for hydropower and relatively large reserves of natural gas. The share of natural gas reserves in the Asia Pacific countries is 8.2 percent at the end of 2007 compared to 3.3 percent of oil reserves.[7] A study on regional cooperation and energy development in the Greater Mekong sub-region shows that the total exploitable hydro potential (168,000MW) is more than 15 times of the installed capacity (11,204MW) in the region in 2001 (Yu, 2003).[8] To turn this potential into reality, a regional power grid-based market needs to be established as one country cannot afford the total costs required for the development. Moreover the country may not be able to absorb the entire amount of electricity supply produced by their hydro potential.

Natural gas is more abundant in the region compared to crude oil as noted above. Total reserves of natural gas are enough for consumption by the countries in the region for more than 40 years assuming the current level of consumption is sustained and the reserves are used only in the region.[9] This could imply that it

---

[7] BP Statistical Review of World Energy 2008. For the Asia Pacific region, countries include mainly Australia, Bangladesh, Brunei, China, India, Indonesia, Malaysia, Myanmar, Pakistan, Papua New Guinea, Thailand, and Vietnam.

[8] The Greater Mekong Sub-region (GMS) consists of Cambodia, Laos, Myanmar, Thailand, Vietnam and the Yunnan province of China.

[9] The reserve-production ratio for Asia-Pacific is about two thirds of a reserve-production ratio for world proved reserves of natural gas. The ratio is far larger than that for North America but smaller than that for other regions like South and Central America, the Middle East, and Africa. The world total proved reserves of natural gas are 179.83 trillion cubic meters and for Asia Pacific, 14.84 trillion cubic meters at the end of 2005.

would bring benefits to the region if a supply chain for natural gas in the region is connected via pipelines or liquefied natural gas (LNG) terminals and tankers. A Pan-Asian natural gas trade model shows that there would be net gains among traders in the region if full-fledged gas trade networks are implemented (Chang and Pan, 2006). Though this is done based on a hypothetical setting, this would support or strengthen the prospects of an integrated energy market in the region. Along with this line, how the proposed Trans-ASEAN Gas Pipeline could help launch an integrated energy market could be examined. "The Pan-Asian gas trade model" including countries in the Middle East, ASEAN, and East Asia such as Japan, China, and Korea, and Russia shows that a full-fledged gas trade would lower the general price level in the region and increase trade volume, but a few countries would have to face higher prices than before the establishment of full-fledged gas trade.

Efforts for Launching an Integrated Energy Market in ASEAN

Energy security — supplying energy in a reliable and stable way at a reasonable price — has been approached somewhat collectively in ASEAN since 1986 when the ASEAN Petroleum Security Agreement was signed in Manila with six states as parties (Lye and Chang, 2004).

Table 6.1 presents the status of energy availability and consumption in the region such as fossil fuel reserves and the level of fossil fuel consumption. There is a huge imbalance — the level of consumption in the region vs the amount of indigenous supply — in oil and natural gas while relatively large surplus of coal in the region.

Apart from the availability of resources and resource imbalance, there are a few measures to examine the status of energy diversification which could indicate the status of energy security. Table 6.2 shows the level of energy diversification in the ASEAN and the level of energy security inferred from the diversification measures.

Table 6.1:   The status of fossil fuels in ASEAN.

Country	Reserves			Cons (mtoe)		
	Oil (tmt)	NG (tcm))	Coal (mt)	Oil	NG	Coal
Brunei	0.2	0.34	—	0.6	1.6	—
Cambodia	—	—	—	0.2	—	—
Indonesia	0.6	3.0	4,328	54.4	30.4	27.8
Lao PDR	—	—	—	0.2	—	—
Malaysia	0.7	2.48	—	23.6	25.4	6.9
Myanmar	—	0.6	—	1.7	2.2	—
Philippines	—	—	—	13.9	3.1	5.9
Singapore	—	—	—	47.4	5.9	—
Thailand	0.1	0.33	1,354	43.0	31.8	8.9
Vietnam	0.5	0.22	150	13.0	4.5	10.4
Total	14.9	6.97	5,832	198	104.9	59.9

Source: BP World Statistical Review of World Energy (2008).

Table 6.2:   The status of energy diversification.

Country	Number of resources (n)	Most utilized (%)	Share of fossil fuels (%)	Share of top 5 (%)
Brunei	0.5 (2)	NG (73)	100.0	100
Cambodia	1.0 (1)	Oil (100)	100.0	100
Indonesia	0.11 (9)	Oil (47)	97.7	99.6
Lao PDR	0. 33 (3)	Oil (100)	100.0	100
Malaysia	0.13 (8)	NG (51)	97.5	100*
Myanmar	0.5 (2)	NG (56)	100.0	100
Philippines	0.13 (8)	Oil (58)	92.5	100*
Singapore	0.33 (3)	Oil (88)	100.0	100
Thailand	0.13 (8)	Oil (52)	96.6	98.1
Vietnam	0.17 (6)	Oil (37)	100*	100*

Source: Author's Calculations.

The first measure is the inverse of the number of energy resources utilized (i.e., $1/n$ where n is the number of energy resources used in a country). This is an overall indicator; it is simple and straightforward. The lower the value is, the better the status of energy security. The share of the most utilized resource (%) is the second type, which shows the degree of dominant resource or the level of concentration. The lower value could indicate the better level of energy security because the dependence of one resource is not severe or critical. The share of fossil fuels used (%) is a variety of the measure based on the most utilized resource and it shows the dependence on fossil fuels. The lower value of this measure reflects the better status of an economy in terms of energy security because this indicates the higher level availability of non-fossil fuels that are generally non-depletable. The most reliable or direct measure is the share of top 5 most utilized resources (%) that could reflect true and relative energy diversity as the five most utilized resources must include resources other than fossil fuels that count only up to three. With this measure, the lower value could mean the better status of an economy in terms of energy security.

Table 6.3 shows that, like the lower level of fossil fuel reserves, the level of renewable energy utilization in the ASEAN is also minimal. Unlike the low and poor availability of fossil fuels in the region, however, Table 6.4 presents the huge potential of

Table 6.3:   Renewable energy utilized in ASEAN.

Country	Hydro (MW)	Wind (MW)	Solar (MW)	Geotheraml (MW)	Biomass (MW)
Brunei	–	–	2.4 kW	–	–
Cambodia	21	–	700 kW	–	–
Indonesia	4,264	0.5	5	802	312
Laos	2,143	–	285 kV	–	
Malaysia	2,066	0.15	150 MWp; 450 kWp	–	211
Myanmar	–	–	–	–	–
Philippines	2,867	1.18	1	1,931	–
Singapore	–	–	90 kWp	–	220
Thailand	139	0.5	6	1	560
Vietnam	220	–	0.6	–	50

Source: Lidula *et al.* (2007).

Table 6.4: Renewable energy potential in ASEAN.

Country	Hydro (MW)	Wind (MW)	Solar PV (kWh/m²/day)	Geothermal (MW)	Biomass (MW)
Brunei	–	–	No information	–	–
Cambodia	Technical 300 (mini/micro/Pico) 10,000 (large)	Theoretical 1,300 (7–8m/s) 120 (8–9m/s)	5 (6–9h)		Technical 700
Indonesia	Technical 75,000 (large) 459 (mini/micro)	Theoretical Significant (3–6m/s)	4.8	Technical 27,000	Technical 49,810
Lao PDR	Theoretical 26,500 Technical 18,000	Theoretical 24,000 (7–8m/s) 2.7 (8–9m/s)	4.5–4.7		
Malaysia	Technical 29,000 (large)	Some small islands	4.5		Technical 29,000
Myanmar	–	–	–	–	–

(*Continued*)

Table 6.4: (*Continued*)

Country	Hydro (MW)	Wind (MW)	Solar PV (kWh/m²/day)	Geothermal (MW)	Biomass (MW)
Philippines	Technical 11,223 (large & small) 1,847 (mini) 27 (micro)	Theoretical 76,600 Technical 7,404	5.1	2,600	Commercial 20
Singapore	—		No information		Wood waste
Thailand	Technical 700 (small)	Theoretical 3,000 (7–8 m/s) 52 (8–9 m/s) Technical 1,600	5.1	5.3	Technical 7,000
Vietnam	Technical 800–1,400 (small) 90–150 (Pico) 300–600 (isolated mini-grid) 400–600 (grid-based mini)	Theoretical 103,000 (7–8 m/s) 8.7 (8–9 m/s) Technical 452 (> 9 m/s)	5 (4–5.9h)	Technical 200–340	Technical 400

Source: Lidula *et al.* (2007).

renewable energy such as hydropower, wind, solar energy, geothermal and biomass in the region.

Given the huge potential in hydropower and other renewable energy, there have been various initiatives and developments in energy cooperation and programs in the region. Notable are the Programme of Action for Enhancement of ASEAN Cooperation on Energy in 1990, the ASEAN Vision 2020 adopted by the Heads of State/Government of the ASEAN in 1997 and the establishment of the ASEAN Centre for Energy in 1999. The ASEAN Vision 2020 envisioned the region being "freed from nuclear weapons in the region". It also announced the establishing of interconnecting arrangements in the field of energy and utilities for electricity, natural gas and water within ASEAN through the ASEAN Power Grid and a Trans-ASEAN Gas Pipeline and Water Pipeline, and promoting cooperation in energy efficiency and conservation, as well as the development of new and renewable energy resources.

The ASEAN Centre for Energy has helped prepare the ASEAN Plan of Action for Energy Cooperation for 1999–2004. It facilitates and coordinates the work of specialist organizations such as the Forum of Heads of ASEAN Power Utilities/Authorities (HAPUA), the ASEAN Council on Petroleum (ASCOPE), the ASEAN Forum on Coal, the Energy Efficiency and Conservation Sub-sector Network, and the New and Renewable Sources of Energy Sub-sector Network. ASCOPE was tasked to lead the ASEAN Power Grid and the Trans-ASEAN Gas Pipeline (TAGP) projects to enhance greater energy security in the region. It established a TAGP Task Force in November 1998, which reviewed and formulated a master plan. The master plan was completed in April 2001 and identified seven possible interconnections for full integration of the pipeline network in ASEAN with a total investment of some US$7 billion. An ASEAN Gas Consultative Council has been established to serve as an advisory body to ASCOPE in the implementation of the TAGP Project in July 2002.

The ASEAN Plan of Action for Energy Cooperation 1999–2004 focuses on six program areas: the ASEAN Power Grid; the Trans-ASEAN Gas Pipeline; Coal, Energy Efficiency and Conservation;

Table 6.5: The planned hydropower developments in the GMS.

Hydro project	Year	Origin	Destination	Installed capacity (MW)	Firm capacity (MW)
Nam Theun 2	2008	Lao PDR	Thailand	1,088	937
Nam Ngum	2008	Lao PDR	Thailand	615	415
Xe Pian-Xe Namnoy	2010	Lao PDR	Thailand	390	362
Xe Khaman 1	2010	Lao PDR	Thailand	468	408
Tasang	2012	Myanmar	Thailand	3,600	3,000
Jinhong	2013	China	Thailand	1,500	863
Nuozhadu	2014	China	Thailand	5,500	2,393
Sambor CPEC	2019	Cambodia	Vietnam	465	347

Source: APERC (2004).

New and Renewable Sources of Energy; Regional Energy Outlook; Energy Policy and Environmental Analysis. Table 6.5 shows the status of hydropower development in the GMS (both planned and designed) and the usefulness of such hydropower developments would be strengthened when the ASEAN Power Grid is completed. Table 6.6 shows how the ASEAN Power Grid is interconnected. As the successor plan to the APAEC 1999–2004, the ASEAN Plan of Action for Energy Cooperation 2004–2009 has been finalized for adoption by the 22nd ASEAN Ministers on Energy Meeting (AMEM) in June 2004. It will enhance the integration of the regional energy infrastructures, promote energy security, create responsive policies to progressively enhance market reforms and liberalization, as well as on the sustainability of the environment. The Plan consists of sectoral plans of action and roadmaps related to the ASEAN Power Grid; TAGP; Energy Efficiency and Conservation; New and Renewable Sources of Energy and Regional Energy Policy and Planning.

Beyond cooperation at the ASEAN level, the First ASEAN Ministers of Energy Meeting +3 (AMEM+3) was held in 2004 and announced a joint declaration to strengthen energy infrastructure-building in the region. The Second AMEM+3 meeting was held in

Table 6.6:   Status of Southeast Asian power grid interconnection projects.

Interconnection project	Type	Capacity (MW)	Status, start
1. Thailand − Lao PDR	HVAC PP	2015/1578	AP 2008/2010
2. Thailand − Myanmar	HVAC PP	1500	AP 2013
3. Thailand − Cambodia	HVAC EE	300	AP 2016
4. Lao PDR − Vietnam	HVAC PP	1887	AP 2007/2016
5. Vietnam − Cambodia	HVAC PP	80/120	UC 2003/2006
6. Peninsula Malaysia − Sumatra	HVDC EE	600	UC 2008
7. Peninsula Malaysia − Singapore	HVAC PP	700	Planned 2012
8. Sumatra − Singapore	HVAC PP	600	Planned 2014
9. Batam (Indonesia) − Singapore	HVAC PP	200/200/200	UC 2014/15/17
10. Sabah/Sarawak − Brunei	HVAC EE	300	Planned 2019
11. Sarawak − W. Kalimantan	HVAC EE	300	Planned 2007
12. Thailand − Peninsula Malaysia	Undecided	Undecided	Speculative
13. Peninsula Malaysia − Sarawak	Undecided	Undecided	Speculative
14. Sabah − Philippines	Undecided	Undecided	Speculative
15. Lao PDR − Cambodia	Undecided	Undecided	Speculative

Source: APERC (2004).

2005 whose theme was "Promoting Greater Energy Stability, Security and Sustainability through ASEAN+3 Energy Partnership". Another geographical extension of cooperation was made during the First ASEAN–Russian Federation Summit in Kuala Lumpur in December 2005. The Summit announced a joint statement stressing the need to "undertake collective initiatives to ensure stable energy supplies through large-scale development of alternative and renewable energy sources, intensifying oil and gas exploration and the promotion of energy conservation and energy efficiency".

Recently, with regard to an integrated energy market, PM Lee Hsien Loong had spoken about the merits of integrated regional energy at the East Asia Summit (EAS) in Cebu in mid-January 2007. His views were supported by the other EAS Leaders, and they decided to encourage "the development of open and competitive regional energy markets geared towards providing affordable energy at all economic levels". (The EAS member countries comprise all 10 ASEAN members plus China, Japan, Korea, India, Australia and New Zealand.)

An outline about how an integrated regional market on energy can benefit countries in the region has been presented at the EAS. With ensuring efficient energy supplies at affordable prices as a key objective of energy policy, EAS has identified the establishment of efficient and flexible international and regional energy markets as an important strategy to achieve the stated goal in the long term. (The energy market was framed in the context of the EAS geographical footprint. But discussion might not be limited to launching an integrated energy market in the EAS region. If the region becomes large, it would only make integration much more challenging.) According to the economic theory introduced in the first paragraph of this chapter, when individuals or countries form a coalition or trade among themselves, it would bring benefits to them. However, when the number of participants gets larger, there might be an empty in the core, i.e., no coalition is formed or no trade occurs so that no benefits are accrued to the participants. This possibility of having an empty core must be avoided when a coalition is formed especially in the early stage. The optimal number of participants is not verified yet, but it must be large enough for accruing mutual benefits and small enough so that the possibility of an empty core is avoided. The progress of talks under international agreements such as Doha Round or the Kyoto Protocol has shown how difficult it is for a large coalition to bring benefits, let alone reach mutual agreement on issues discussed.

Given the possibility of the empty core, we could start to form an integrated energy market on a relatively small scale between 10 to 20 countries. Second, the scope of the integrated energy market must be transparent and straightforward. For example, the utmost goal could be providing electricity at the lowest cost possible without being influenced by market power and/or distorted by political discord. These efforts must be pursued in the framework of "cooperative competition" in which the cooperative efforts to increase an economic pie are collectively pursued while the pursuit of increasing the market share of each country is made individually and competitively.

As mentioned earlier, there are three movements that have made cooperative efforts to build an integrated energy market in the region with or without economic cooperation and development. These are the Greater Mekong Sub-region (GMS) economic cooperation and development, ASEAN Power Grid (APG) and Trans-ASEAN Gas Pipeline (TAGP). The GMS has formed a sub-regional economic cooperation program in 1992 aided by the Asian Development Bank. The program has helped the countries in the region achieve economic growth, but its potential for economic growth has not been fully utilized.

As shown in Table 6.4, there have been cooperation efforts in the Greater Mekong Sub-region (GMS). ADB initiated a technical assistance program for promoting sub-regional cooperation among Cambodia, the PRC, Lao PDR, Myanmar, Thailand and Vietnam in 1992. An Electric Power Forum was established by the GMS Ministerial Conference in Yangoon in April 1995. Sub-regional power projects such as Theun Hinboun and Houay Ho in Lao PDR (to Thailand) and Nam Leuk Hydropower Project in Lao PDR had been started and the latter is now exporting power to Thailand. Feasibility studies in the GMS have been done as well. A sub-regional Energy Sector Study provided initial guidelines for regional power developments such as Se Kong-Se San and Nam Theun River Basin Hydropower Development. Mekong Integrated Transmission Study financed by JICA and ADB and implemented by the Mekong River Commission Secretariat. Power Trade Strategy Study was carried out by the World Bank. Feasibility studies on Nam Theun 2, Nam Ngum 2, Nam Ngum 3, and Jin Hong Hydropower Projects have been done. Examination of establishing a national grid company in the Lao PDR, and the Nam Ngum 500 kV Transmission Project has been done. Expert Group on Power

Interconnection and Trade was established to facilitate cross-border power trade and to advise on adoption of a Policy Statement. From these experiences of energy developments in the GMS, five principles of cooperation were suggested: Implementation, Policies, Social Acceptability, Sharing of Benefits, Costs and Risks, and Project Issues (Chander, 2000).

Since the first mainstream dam, Manwan (1,500MW), was built in Yunnan, China in 1995, there are various projects under implementation or are being studied. However, the main concern now is not economic viability of building hydro dams per se but the long-term environmental impact of dam-building. A cascade of dams on the Mekong River or China's hydropower plans affect countries the downstream in terms of falling water levels, declining fish stock, and rising salinity levels. But building hydropower dams seems to be the most feasible solution for ensuring energy security (Dosch and Hensengerth, 2005).

After completing an interconnection master plan in March 2003, steps needed to make the APG fully workable have been identified and more efforts have been made to operate it at full scale. But there are obstacles in commercial justification and availability of funding. Even though very tangible benefits have accrued from the APG, the memorandum of understanding (MOU) on the APG was argued only in 2007. As for the TAGP, the MOU on TAGP was signed in July 2002 and joint studies on cross-border issues such as tariffs, transit rights and security of supply are expected to be facilitated. The establishments of AGP and TAGP in ASEAN are considered groundbreaking step for launching an integrated energy market in the region. But the slowness in developing further enhancement of a common infrastructure for electricity and natural gas in the region proves that there are various obstacles to be cleared before a full-blown and well-functioning integrated energy market can be launched. Launching an integrated energy market is not only a long-term goal but a short-term target that can be met via forming an integrated energy market with a small group or on a small scale such as a coalition of three to four countries for sharing electricity or natural gas.

The necessity, feasibility and plausibility of establishing an integrated regional energy market has found consensus among the interested countries. The initial clearance for proceeding with the integrated market such as MOUs has been made. However, the consensus on some critical factors such as financial and cost-sharing and political will has not been reached yet. A viable option on a small scale must be identified and pursued first as the EU had started from cooperative efforts on a small scale for coal and steel.

There have been latest developments in regional cooperation on energy. Civilian Usage of Nuclear Energy was adopted in 20 November 2007 in Singapore. The ASEAN Declaration on Environmental Sustainability declares to forge "ASEAN-wide cooperation to establish a regional nuclear safety regime". As recently as March 2009, Voluntary Stockpiling Efforts have been done. ASEAN Petroleum Security Agreement (APSA) during ASEAN Summit in Thailand on 26 February to 1 March 2009 included voluntary oil stockpiling as one of the medium- and long-term measures (Article 3.3[f]). Although the ASEAN Petroleum Security Agreement signed recently in Thailand marks a milestone for ensuring regional energy security by including a provision for voluntary oil stockpiles, Chang and Koh (2009) assert that mandatory, as opposed to voluntary, oil stockpiling could better serve the medium- and long-term energy security needs of ASEAN.

Quantification of Effects from Integrated Energy Market in the Region

There are various studies that examined the possible (positive) effects from integrated energy market in the region as shown in Table 6.7. A study focusing on integrated energy planning for ASEAN countries and Southern China (Yu *et al.*, 2006) examined network topology, ASEAN–Yunnan generation capacity, natural gas potential, generation potential, new generation — proposed, international transmission capacity — proposed and cost savings/comparisons. They find run-of-river hydropower plants bring benefits and

Table 6.7: Summary of effects from integrated energy market.

Study	Authors (year)	Findings
Integrated Energy Planning in ASEAN.	Yu *et al.* (2006).	Cost savings from run-of-river schemes.
Pan-Asian Gas Trade.	Chang and Pan (2006).	Benefits from increased trade links and competition.
Energy Integration in the Greater Mekong Sub-region.	ADB (2008).	Integration could deliver secure, sustainable and competitive energy.
Cross-Border Power Trade.	Watcharejyothin and Shrestha (2009).	Lower energy system costs and better environmental quality.

greater cost savings but have smaller impacts on the ecological system in the region. Hence, they suggest that run-of-river schemes be a top policy priority for energy planners in the region.

As mentioned earlier, Pan-Asian Gas Trade Model (Chang and Pan, 2006) finds Asian gas markets are currently inadequately developed to function effectively in a competitive framework. But it would benefit from increased trade links and competition. Russia is a key player in the development of a fully integrated Pan-Asian natural gas market and lowers the average price of natural gas in the region.

The ADB Study on Energy Integration in the GMS (ADB, 2008) finds the region as a whole is well-endowed with necessary energy resources. But the resources are unevenly distributed. Hydropower potentials are great in countries like Lao PDR, Myanmar and Yunnan Province, gas resources are relatively abundant in Thailand and Myanmar and coal reserves are plenty in Vietnam and Yunnan Province. In view of these characteristics, it asserts an integrated approach is needed to deliver sustainable, secure and competitive energy.[10]

---

[10] Asian Development Bank: *Building a Sustainable Energy Future: The Greater Mekong Subregion*, 2008, is still a discussion draft and asked "Not to be quoted".

Watcharejyothin and Shrestha (2009) examine the plausibility and feasibility of cross-border power trade between Laos and Thailand in an energy-economy model. Effects of hydropower development in Laos and power trade between Laos and Thailand appear not to be small. Eighty percent exploitation of water resource in Laos would induce power trade between the two countries while the integrated energy system costs would decrease marginally and CO_2 emissions would decrease by two percent. Thailand, a net importer, would get benefits — lower energy system cost, better environmental quality, greater diversification of energy sources while Laos, a net exporter, would get benefits — significant export revenues, increased profitability of revenue and energy system cost from the maximum exploitation of hydropower resource.

Concluding Remarks

This chapter explores how global economic crises could drive cooperative efforts and integration of energy markets to ensure energy security in a region by reviewing what has been done with integrated energy markets in the world and examining the possibility, plausibility and obstacles of launching an integrated energy market in the region. The common European market could shed some light on how the region can launch an integrated energy market. An integrated electricity network in West Africa is expected to bring some benefits such as lower electricity supply cost and enhanced system reliability to the countries linked to the network. A pan-Asian natural gas trade model also postulates that net gains would be possible under a full-fledged trade framework in which all countries are connected via either gas pipelines or LNG terminals and tankers. Cross-border power trade in the region would bring benefits that could far exceed the costs of making such trade possible.

A few movements in economic cooperation and energy development such as Greater Mekong Sub-region economic cooperation and energy development, the ASEAN Power Grid and the

Trans-ASEAN Gas Pipeline could be considered initial steps to launch an integrated energy market in the region. Energy market integration spearheaded in the East Asia Summit in January 2007 would spur the movements towards launching an integrated energy market in the region. It could be said that the region has put appropriate efforts to pave a way towards introducing an integrated energy market in the region. The specific ways to make an integrated energy market fully operational in the region requires more feasibility studies and cooperative efforts among the parties involved in forming a coalition for such a market along with firm political will and robust economic drivers.

There is some progress in cooperative efforts to improve energy security in the region which has started in the 1990s. However, they are still mere discussions, meetings and agreements and the level of realization out of such efforts is very low, if not nil. The European Union's experiences show that the full integration takes a long time and many obstacles and huddles have to be overcome. ASEAN, as an integrated community, can take lessons from those experiences and suggest implementation plans that could avoid delays and barriers.

References

Asia Pacific Energy Research Centre (2004). *Electric Power Grid Interconnections in the APEC Region.* Japan.

Chander, S. (2000). South-Asia Growth Quadrangle Cooperation in the Energy Sector. Mimeograph. Asian Development Bank.

Chang, Y. H. and C. Koh (2009). Asean Petroleum Security Agreement: Sealed or Leaking? *RSIS Commentary.* S. Rajaratnam School of International Studies, Nanyang Technological University.

Chang, Y. H. and T. Pan (2006). Pan-Asian gas trade model in competitive market frameworks. Proceedings of the market frameworks. Proceedings of the 26th USAEE/IAEE North American Conference, Ann Arbor, Michigan, USA.

Chang, Y. H. and T. Pan (2006). Pan–Asian Gas Trade Model. Mimeograph. National University of Singapore.

Domanico, F. (2007). Concentration in the European Electricity Industry: The Internal Market as Solution? *Energy Policy,* 35, pp. 5064–5076.

Dosch, J. and O. Hensengerth (2005). Sub-regional Cooperation in Southeast Asia: The Mekong Basin. *EJEAS,* 4(2), pp. 263–285.

Gnansounou, E., H. Bayem, D. Bednyagin and J. Deng (2007). Strategies for Regional Integration of Electricity Supply in West Africa. *Energy Policy,* 35, pp. 4142–4153.

Larsen, A., L. H. Pedersen, E. M. Sorensen and O. J. Olsen (2006). Independent Regulatory Authorities in European Electricity Markets. *Energy Policy,* 34, pp. 2858–2870.

Lidula, N. W. A., N. Mithulananthan, W. Ongsakul, C. Widjaya and R. Henson (2007). ASEAN towards Clean and Sustainable Energy: Potentials, Utlization and Barriers. *Renewable Energy,* 32, 1441–1452.

Lise, W., B. F. Hobbs and S. Hers (2008). Market Power in the European Electricity Market — The Impacts of Dry Weather and Additional Transmission Capacity. *Energy Policy,* 36, 1331–1343.

Lye, L. H. and Y. H. Chang (2004). Singapore: National energy security and regional cooperation. In B. Barton, C. Redgwell, A. Ronne and D. N. Zillman (eds), *Energy Security: Managing Risk in a Dynamic Legal and Regulatory Environment,* Oxford University Press.

Watcharejyothin, M. and R. Shrestha (2009). Effects of cross-border power trade between Laos and Thailand: Energy security and environmental implications. *Energy Policy* (forthcoming).

Yu, X. J. (2003). Regional Cooperation and Energy Development in the Greater Mekong Sub-region. *Energy Policy,* 30, pp. 1221–1224.

Yu, Z., B. H. Bowen, F. T. Sparrow, V. Siriariyaporn and L. Yu (2006). Integrated Energy Resources Planning for the ASEAN Countries and Southern China. *Oil, Gas & Energy Law Intelligence,* 3(4), pp. 1–12.

PART II

ECONOMIC AND POLICY ISSUES

CHAPTER 7

Singapore Growth Model: Its Strengths and Its Weaknesses*

LIM CHONG YAH

This chapter postulates that the Singapore growth and development model rests on five premises: (1) market orientation, (2) foreign trade orientation, (3) high savings and high investment, (4) macroeconomic stability, and (5) stable and sound public governance. The subsets of each of the five pillars are then elaborated. The lecture also enumerates the impressive successes of the model and then concludes with the Achilles' heels of the system: (1) deterioration in the Gini coefficient, (2) vulnerability to external shocks and (3) de-population consequence and problem.

The Development Model

What constitutes the Singapore model of growth and development? In my view, the model has five basic parts, the removal

---

* Lecture presented at the NTU–MOE Seminar 2009 at NTU on 14 March 2009 to Junior College students of economics in Singapore.

of any of which would collapse the whole model. The five basic foundations are:

(1) market orientation,
(2) foreign trade orientation,
(3) high savings and high investment,
(4) macroeconomic stability, and
(5) stable and sound public governance.

We shall now look at each pillar in greater detail. Also, when a set or subset malfunctions, the whole system may dysfunction, growth decelerates and unemployment accelerates. The model is built on the small but strategic location of Singapore with a small multi-ethnic population of only four to five million at the end or beginning of the Straits of Malacca.

(1) *Market Orientation*

This is based on three fundamental freedoms:

(1) freedom of private property ownership,
(2) freedom of private enterprise, and
(3) freedom of exchange of goods and services.

Market forces of supply and demand determine the nature and composition of national and company input for output in production and for exchange. There is also a strong preference for inducement (monetary incentives and disincentives) to direction. Production and consumption quotas and targets for individuals and firms are eschewed. Society produces for the markets which decide on what to produce, how much to produce, where to produce and the prices of the products. In Singapore price-fixing is eschewed, including for food and for fuel. There is a maximum of economic freedom. This may also be called *perestroika* or economic reform or economic freedom; a maximum and an optimum of *perestroika*.

However, it does not mean that the markets in Singapore, such as the stock market, have no rules and no regulations. Without the necessary minimum of rules, the markets can become chaotic and anarchic. Functioning markets are ensured, established and cherished.

(2) *Foreign Trade Orientation*

No man is an island unto itself, so are nation-states in a globalized world. That Singapore is small geographically and in terms of population make it more pertinent for Singapore to engage extensively in international trade and international exchange of ideas, knowledge and technology. In a word, Singapore was founded and survives on Free Trade. Singapore buys from the cheapest markets and sells to the dearest, not just in the region but also in the world.

The theory of comparative advantage compels Singapore to specialize which, in fact, means to depend very largely on the outside world for imports as well as for exports. Any economic **autarkic** policy will ruin Singapore, as any political and social isolation will bring her to her knees. The average and the marginal propensity to import are very high.

In foreign trade, Singapore survives, if not prospers as well. The volume of foreign merchandise trade Singapore handles is thus quite staggering. It is bigger than all the well-known countries in the whole of the Indian sub-continent combined, even when the important **entrepot trade** is excluded (Lim, 2009a, pp. 17–18).

More than that, as a financial centre, Singapore also depends on capital inflow and outflow as a part of the routine function. And, of course, trade means not just visible trade but also invisible trade. Besides, as the internal market is small, FDI and much of local investment depend on the global market right from inception. Straightaway, they have to face the full blast of international competition. There is no import substitution or export substitution policy. There are no export taxes, nor import taxes, except on a few "sinful" products like tobacco and alcohol.

(3) *High Savings and High Investment Strategy*

In a closed economy, high investment can take place only if there is a high savings function. In an open economy such as Singapore's, FDI inflow increases investment and investments thus can exceed savings. Singapore has both high domestic savings as well as high net FDI inflow, making her real growth rates very high, at an average of 8.1 percent per annum for the last 43 years since Independence in 1965 (Lim, 2009a, pp. 5–6).

The following growth equation taken from Harrod and Domar emphasizes the importance of the savings function in generating economic growth through investment growth. In the case of Singapore, domestic investment growth has been very much augmented by FDI inflow.

$$\frac{\Delta Y}{Y} = \frac{S}{Y} \cdot \frac{\Delta Y}{I}$$

Harrod points out in Chapter 4 of his book, *Economic Dynamics*, that the equation is a truism, a very important truism like MV = PT in Fisher's Equation of Exchange. Growth rate ($\Delta Y/Y$), the equation states, is a direct function of savings (S/Y), given the inverse of the capital-output ratio ($\Delta Y/I$). In other words, the equation states that without savings, there can be no growth.

The overall savings function in fact can be decomposed into private sector and public sector savings, and both are very high in Singapore. Private sector savings consist of (1) household and personal savings, (2) corporate savings and (3) in Singapore, also CPF savings. Contrary to popular belief, CPF savings constitute only a small portion of the national savings in Singapore, though it is a very important one to most contributors. Corporate savings are the main savings in the private sector. It means companies in Singapore are on the whole very profitable. Public sector savings refer to the annual Government budget surpluses and surpluses of statutory boards like the PSA (Port of Singapore Authority). The huge surpluses of the very important and ubiquitous Government-linked corporations like Singapore Airlines, the Development Bank of Singapore (DBS), SingTel and Sembcorp Marine are shown in the private sector company surpluses, as they are run like private corporations (Lim, 2008; Ramirez and Tan, 2003).

In other words, if a country has a very low savings function, it may imply that the public sector is in persistent deficit and the private sector surplus is so low that it cannot wipe out the public sector deficit.

In Singapore, private sector investment outnumber public sector investment by a ratio of 5 to 1 (Hsieh, 2002).

Actually, investment should mean not just investment in physical capital, which is the normal concept and normal usage of investment, but also investment in human capital, investment in social capital and investment in natural capital. The Singapore model also depends heavily on investment in human capital and investment in social capital. On human capital, for example, at the time of Independence in 1965, only six percent of the primary school cohorts could have access to higher education. In 2004, this went up to 67 percent.

Investment in social capital in Singapore means the effective promotion of inter-religious and inter-racial harmony in a multi-racial, multi-lingual and multi-religious society. It also means serious investment in tripartism or working together among the three social partners: the Government, the employers and the trade unions or organized labor. The successful tripartite bodies which I am most familiar with are the National Wages Council (NWC) and the Skills Development Fund (SDF) Advisory Council (Lim and Chew, 1998).

(4) *Macroeconomic Stability*

Macroeconomic stability is based on three premises. One, a stable internal value of money. Two, a stable external value of money. Three, a balanced budget in the Government.

A stable internal value of money in a market-oriented economy in effect means a low and stable CPI (consumer price index). To achieve this objective, money supply has to be properly regulated. The following equation is helpful: $\pi = \dot{m} - \dot{y} + \dot{v}$. π is the rate of inflation. $\dot{m}$ is the rate of increase in the quantity of money. $\dot{y}$ is the rate of increase in national income and $\dot{v}$ the rate of increase in velocity of circulation of money. Given $\dot{v}$, if $\dot{m}$ exceeds $\dot{y}$, inflation results. $\dot{v}$ may add to the inflationary or deflationary momentum in a circular cumulative causation process.

In a small, very open economy like Singapore, the exchange rate (the external value of money) also plays an important role in the determination of π, the rate of inflation. A depreciation of the exchange rate increases π and an appreciation decreases π. Because the exchange rate cuts both ways in import and export prices, it is not used and cannot be used in Singapore to enhance external competitiveness. It is used essentially as a means of external payment.

There is no specific inflation rate or exchange rate targeting in Singapore. This is because prices of imports are out of the control of Singapore. Similarly, the exchange rates of other countries are outside the control of Singapore. And yet, both import prices and external exchange rates affect greatly the internal and external value of the Singapore dollar. Our exchange rate, in parenthesis, is based on a basket of exchange rates of our important trading partners. We follow the so-called BBC system in exchange rate management (Wilson, 2009). BBC means "bracket", "band" and "crawl".

Through prudent and able budgetary management, Singapore normally has a budget surplus, which is set aside for a rainy day. This surplus is achieved despite persistent and constant lowering of taxes, particularly direct taxes on wage income and profit. In part this budget surplus is attributable to the benefit of rapidly rising national income over the years, in part attributable to a good system of tax collection, and in part the use of other alternative taxes, such as GST to augment tax collection.

Because of budget surpluses, the Government does not have to resort to foreign borrowing or to fiduciary issue, a pseudonym for the printing of money.

The CPF system too contributes to macroeconomic stability through channelling of compulsory savings for public housing, healthcare needs and minimum old-age provision. In these provisions, there is no pooling of resources: each contributor keeps and builds up his or her own account. The compulsory contributions are free from tax (Chew and Chew, 2009).

(5) *Stable and Sound Public Administration*

This is based on the existence of a credible, stable and able, development-oriented government since Independence in 1965, really since self-government in 1959. It is also based on a sound, stable, effective, non-corrupt civil service system. This sound and able public service system has been deliberately built up and nurtured by the political leadership. It is meritocratically-based, and public servants are justly remunerated, bearing in mind competing market demand for talents in a fast-growing economy. Law and order and a good, efficient and impartial judiciary have been valued and fostered. They form an integral part of good public governance, besides the protection of property and other individual and family rights.

World-class public goods and services, too, have been made available to all as an integral part of the good public administration system and as an indispensable support for overall social and economic development.

That Singapore has the same Government throughout the period since self-government in 1959 has also enabled it to take a long-term view on development, instead of only with a short-term perspective, within the shorter life-span of the elected leadership. Though it has been the same PAP Government, orderly leadership renewal has been deliberately fostered. Continuity and change were discreetly and ably maintained, appearing acceptable to the large majority of the electorate at every periodic General Election.

Strengths of the Model

The growth and development model just described has transformed Singapore from a third world to a first world economy and
society, from a basket-case to a show-case state. Per capital income
in US dollars, grew from $512 in 1965 to $32,624 per annum in 2007
(Lim, 2009a, p. 4). This is attained with price stability, a high savings function, full employment for nearly all the years, a strong
balance on current account and overall balance, and huge accumulation of foreign exchange reserves as well as a stable exchange rate
system, and without any external indebtedness.

Structurally, Singapore has been transformed from an old entrepot trading economy and a British military base East of Suez to an
industrial economy, a regional financial centre, an important oil-
refining hub, an important shipping and civil-aviation hub, a
regional trading emporium, an international tourism centre, as HQ
for MNCs in Southeast Asia and beyond, and an emerging regional
education centre and an emerging healthcare hub (Lim, 2009a, p. 10).

Other social-economic indicators are also impressive:

(1) much longer longevity of life with a very drastic fall in mortal-
    ity rates,
(2) total elimination of ubiquitous slums and absolute poverty,
(3) very impressive spread and improvement in education
    standards,
(4) great strikes in industrial peace and inter-racial and inter-
    religious harmony, and
(5) one of the safest and cleanest cities in the world.

The Achilles' Heels in the Model

(1) *Deterioration in Gini Coefficient*

The impressive success of the model, based on a market-oriented
economy and a meritocratic society, also brings in in its train a
deterioration in the Gini coefficient. It was already high at 0.442 in
2000. It deteriorated further to 0.485 by 2007.

(2) *Vulnerability to External Shocks*

Dependence on the world for its imports, including food and fuel, and also markets for its exports, changes in economic fortunes in the world are easily transmitted to Singapore, often in exaggerated forms. In 1973 and 1974, because of very high import prices of food and fuel, the Consumer Price Index shot up to 20 to 22 percent per year. The Asian financial crisis of 1997–98 also nearly brought Singapore to her knees (Lim, 2009b). The SARS crisis in 2003, too, had its frightening impact on Singapore *(Ibid)*. Currently, the global financial crisis has spread to Singapore with drastic decline in her export income and national income.

(3) *De-population Problem*

The great success of the Singapore model also affected family formation. As more and more women become better and better educated and as more and more of them seek paid employment outside their homes, fertility rates fall. Currently, Singapore cannot replace itself, and yet in 1959, Singapore had one of the highest natural population increases in the world. Kandang Kerbau Hospital was in the Guinness World Records as having the largest baby factory in the world. Today, it is much quieter than it should be: a paucity of pregnant mothers and babies. Society has changed and so has the procreation rate and pattern.

References

Chew, S. B. and R. Chew (2009). Macro Objective of the Central Provident Fund (CPF): A Review. In W. M. Chia and H. Y. Sng (eds.), *Singapore and Asia in a Globalized World: Contemporary Economic Issues and Policies*. World Scientific, pp. 35–62.

Hsieh, C. T. (2002). What Explains the Industrial Revolution in East Asia? Evidence from the Factor Markets. *The American Economic Review*, 92(3).

Lim, C. Y. and R. Chew, (eds.) (1998). *Wages and Wages Policies: Tripartism in Singapore*. World Scientific.

Lim, C. Y. (2008). The Asian Financial Crisis. In *Southeast Asia: The Long Road Ahead* (2nd Ed.). World Scientific.

Lim, C. Y. (2009a). Transformation in the Singapore Economy: Course and Causes. In W. M. Chia and H. Y. Sng (eds.), *Singapore and Asia in a Globalized World: Contemporary Economic Issues and Policies*. World Scientific, pp. 3–23.

Lim, C. Y. (2009b). The Asian Financial Crisis and the Sub-Prime Mortgage Crisis: A Dissenting View. In W. M. Chia and H. Y. Sng (eds.), *Singapore and Asia in a Globalized World: Contemporary Economic Issues and Policies*. World Scientific, pp. 105–120.

Ramirez, C. D. and L. H. Tan (2003). Singapore Inc. Versus the Private Sector: Are Government-Linked Companies Different? IMF Working Paper: WP/03/156.

Wilson, P. (2009). Monetary Policy in Singapore: A BBC Approach. In W. M. Chia and H. Y. Sng (eds.), *Singapore and Asia in a Globalized World: Contemporary Economic Issues and Policies*. World Scientific, pp. 63–86.

CHAPTER 8

The Role of Competition in Singapore: A Complexity Point of View

LAM CHUAN LEONG*

Background

Singaporeans are familiar with the arguments about why we need to be competitive. The only justification for another paper on this subject is the novelty of viewing competition and the underlying free market principle though the lens of complexity science rather than from the purely economic angle. This paper will also underline how public policy here has extensively and consistently applied economic reasoning and competition principles within the limits of public acceptability in pursuit of Singapore's success.

Singapore was founded as a free port in 1819 to compete with ports in the surrounding region. Its tax-free status was a competitive edge and today would have been called a tax incentive. Foreign workers and talent were imported from many areas to provide the skills and ability to make the port a success. In a nutshell,

---

* With assistance from IDA, EMA and CCS. The views expressed here are that of the author and do not represent any view that may be held by the Government of Singapore.

this strategy can hardly be faulted even till today. Singapore's *raison d'etre* from its origin has thus been economic. Even the migrants who set foot here came to seek a better economic life. The lack of a domestic market of significant size meant that Singapore has to be a price-taker in the world market. Without any preferential external market, the only means of surviving well meant being able to sell at the best possible value for money and to import our requirements at the best possible value too; hence the search for competitiveness and efficiency.

The Price Mechanism

Whilst this much of the argument is not too difficult to agree with, the successful inculcation of the competitiveness ethos through public policy measures is what makes for our success. Essentially this has been done through two channels. First is the extensive use of the pricing mechanism in public policy implementation. Second is the laying down of a foundation to allow greater play of market-based competition and using the discipline of the market to drive public sector services such as telecoms and utilities.

Our philosophy has been to leave prices to be determined by a freely competitive market as far as possible. The prices of goods and services provided by the private sector best meet this condition. Goods and services provided by the public sector, however, require some adjustment because the conditions of a competitive market are not completely met. The public sector uses "pricing mechanism" with varying degrees of adjustment for the following services that it provides:

a. Public sector services for which the public pays a part of the full price. This is called public co-payment. This pricing system is used, for example, in health, education, and housing where there are positive externalities.
b. Developmental services, e.g., the government provides partial financial support or incentives for research and development by the private sector, for business promotion, market development

etc. This may be considered a form of public sector co-payment for the positive externalities generated by these activities.

c. Regulatory services e.g., taxes on cars, tobacco products, water which are meant to discourage their consumption and to make the consumer pay for the cost of the negative externalities created by their consumption.

It may be argued that almost every country will have these measures in place. The point worth noting is that Singapore has applied rational economic pricing more extensively and consistently than others. For example, we have used co-payments for health, housing and education to avoid wastage in consumption and to capture the positive externalities involved. However, full market costing is imposed on services such as telecoms, power and water. The latter two services are usually subsidized or underpriced in many other countries.

Similarly, to correct for the negative externalities of road traffic congestion, we prefer to control car population growth and traffic flow using price rather than quotas or rationing. We have avoided schemes like allowing cars to be driven only on alternate days depending on whether the number plate on the car is odd or even because this is a non-price measure. Instead we prefer to use an Electronic Road Pricing system. We have not adopted a rationing system or a ballot system for deciding who should own a car. We use a price-based auction system whereby prospective car-owners have to bid for the right to purchase a car. This system is less liable to be defeated through some "gaming" system. This market-based price competition system for the control of the car population has worked very well since its inception nearly two decades ago.

The Complexity View

The economy as a system may be called a "complex system". A complex system is a one which has a large number of members interacting closely with one another. The economic system comprises many individual human beings and also organizations such as companies, etc. Human beings can learn and change their behavior. Thus a system involving humans can be called a complex adaptive system. Such a system is "innovative". It can create new forms of behavior through a process called "self-organizing".

Viewed as a complex system, it is not surprising that, unless carefully planned, public sector interventions usually result in sub-optimal behavior. No agency or regulator knows enough of the myriad factors and considerations that underlie the behavior of the individual humans within the system. Any rule will tend to become rigid boundaries that prevent the economy from self-organizing to achieve a higher level of optimality. This is amply demonstrated by the failure of even well intentioned central command and control economies. The only way that a complex system can search for a better outcome is for it to have the freedom and flexibility to self-organize around its local environment, to exploit the opportunities and avoid the risks in its immediate neighbourhood. Moreover, such local conditions are transient and change rapidly, too rapidly for externally imposed rules to catch up. This why the "invisible hand" of a liberal market performs better than the rigid barriers created by the regulations of a command economy.

The use of the pricing mechanism is thus highly commended from this point of view because it is not a "rigid" intervention barrier. Consumers can regulate their own behavior around this barrier to maximize their own individual utility functions. If the prices are set based on sound economic reasoning rather than for exploitative or other irrelevant purposes e.g., rent-seeking or to favor any particular vested interest, they become valuable tools in the search for economic efficiency and help move the economy towards a higher level of competitiveness.

An example of this is why rent control in housing usually fails. Rent control tends to end up with an insufficient supply of housing. This defeats the original well-intentioned objective of helping the poor afford housing. Rent control has not played a significant part in Singapore's housing policy. Instead our public housing is made affordable through a system of subsidizing public housing prices relative to the market. The public is incentivized to buy public housing through this subsidy and the availability of self-savings under the Central Provident Fund. This policy has resulted in more than 80 percent of our population owning public housing. Our public housing programme has been a success that has won international acclaim.

In short, the findings of complexity theories fit in well with the philosophy of letting our economy largely function freely on its own. This laissez-faire concept is not an entirely new idea. More than 2000 years ago, Lao Tze commented that "Good government is like frying fish: Do not overdo it." Of course, some regulations and interventions are needed as constraints to ensure that the market system do not enter into a chaotic state. Apart from these constraints, the insight afforded by complexity theories is that other interventions should better be "soft barriers" such as the pricing mechanism rather than "hard barriers" such as quotas or rationing.

The power of self organization is what makes the basic free market model work better than other alternative economic systems during periods when the economy is undergoing relatively slow changes or is in a state of quasi-equilibrium. As a complex system, the economy will never be in a state of complete equilibrium perpetually or there will only be death and no innovation or progress. The free market model allows for changes to be constantly made at the margins by individuals who act independently and continually to adapt to the slowly changing equilibrium. This is why highly regulated economies either do not do as well or they fail catastrophically over time when conditions have moved beyond the circumstances for which the regulations were designed for.

Thinking Ahead of Time

Another feature of Singapore's public policy has been its ability to think well ahead of the time when changes are needed. The examples below are quoted to illustrate this pro-active approach.

Many countries have liberalized or privatized sectors of their economy because either the public agencies providing these services are inefficient or do not have sufficient capital resources to invest in expanding the service to meet growing market demand. The latter is usually due to heavy subsidies which made capital investments unviable. This is common in the telecoms and utilities sectors.

In our case, these are not the reasons that drive our privatization or liberalization policies. It is the search for long term competitiveness through the discipline of the market place that drives these policies. The two examples below will illustrate this.

First is the privatization of the telecoms sector. In 1992, the Telecommunications Authority of Singapore (TAS) was reconstituted as the regulator for the telecommunications sector while its service provisioning arm was corporatized as Singapore Telecommunications or Singtel. At that time, the prevailing technology in telecoms was such that it was considered necessary to allow Singtel to operate as a monopoly at least till 2007. The reasons for corporatization were not driven by inefficiencies in the service provisioning. Rather, it was believed that corporatization would give Singtel greater flexibility and adaptability to face changing market conditions in the future. In the vocabulary of complexity theories, this can be seen as providing Singtel with greater degrees of adaptability to local conditions as a separate agent rather than being part of the larger public sector as a whole. The exercise was also not driven by the ideas of liberalization which were to come later. It was designed to be a move towards a regulated monopoly which could possibly be liberalized later.

However, the speed of technology in the sector proved to be faster than anticipated. The advent of large scale data transmission services especially with the advent of the Internet and the entry and rapid spread of mobile telephony brought about the need to move away from a regulated monopoly structure to a complex market structure in which there are segments where market-based competition can take place effectively. Thus by 2000, the telecoms sector was fully liberalized.

Although Singtel had not been inefficient and was competitively benchmarking its prices against its competitors in the region,

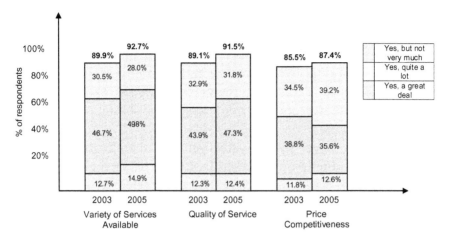

Fig. 8.1: Survey on telecommunication services.

Source: IDA.

Note: Details of the survey results are available at Infocomm Development Authority Website (http://www.ida.gov.sg).

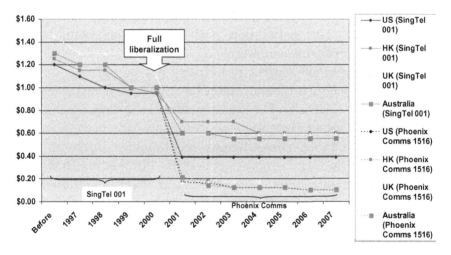

Fig. 8.2: International call prices.

Source: IDA.

the complete liberalization of the sector still brought about significant changes. Figs. 8.1 and 8.2 show that quality of services has risen and prices have dropped as a result of the discipline of the competitive environment brought about by liberalization.

Another example is that of the electricity sector. The Public Utilities Board (PUB) was the sole provider of electricity in Singapore up to the 1990s. This is an example of a vertically integrated utility model based on a central planning system. PUB is responsible for all segments of the value chain, i.e., electricity generation, transmission and distribution and the selling of electricity to end consumers.

Again, the driver for privatization and liberalization for this sector was not due to any marked inefficiencies or inability in the provisioning of these services. PUB was treated as a regulated monopoly because it was thought then that the electricity sector in such a small economy as ours was a "natural monopoly". However, in the 1990s, the UK began looking at forming competitive markets for electricity generation. As Singapore looked ahead at the increasing demand for energy and the possible benefits of competition in contrast to regulation of this sector, it also began to liberalize the sector. By 2000, the national electricity grid which is still viewed as the "natural monopoly" was separated out as a regulated utility. The generation and retailing segments were liberalized and became contestable.

The reform of the electricity industry has brought about real and tangible benefits. Liberalization has put downward pressure on the price of electricity. For example, there are efficiency gains in the generation sector because power companies are incentivized to adopt earlier more cost-efficient technologies such as the Combined Cycle Gas Turbines generators. Competition has also given the companies the impetus to seek to lower operation costs and source for cheaper fuel. The effects can be seen from Fig. 8.3.

It shows that as a result of efficiencies and technological improvements, the companies have been able to keep prices fairly stable despite the recent increase in fuel price. Had we continued with the business-as-before scenario, the prices of electricity would have continued to rise with the fuel price rises. Instead competition amongst the generating companies has kept the tariffs of electricity at a fairly steady level since 2001.

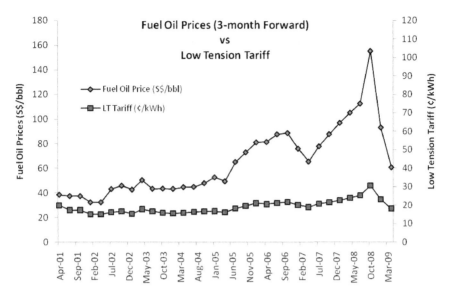

Fig. 8.3: Electricity low tension tariff vs fuel oil prices.

Source: EMA.

In short, this section has demonstrated that in designing the interface between public policy and the private sector, Singapore has been predominantly using the "soft" intervention of the price mechanism to achieve the efficiency goal which is the foundation of competitiveness. In addition, policymakers take a long-term view of efficiency rather than focus merely on fixing immediate problems. Hence long before public sector agencies show any signs of gross inefficiencies or inability to meet their provisioning targets, plans and reforms are put into place to take advantage of better market mechanisms. By subjecting service provisions to the discipline of the market place wherever feasible, Singapore has been able to reap substantial advantages in keeping its competitive edge through greater innovation and efficiency.

The enactment of the Competition Act is yet another example of the government thinking ahead in entrenching innovation and efficiency. Unlike most other countries where such competition laws are enacted partly with an objective to advocate pro-competition government policies, Singapore started with a good foundation of pro-competition culture among most government agencies. Nonetheless, the Competition Act is necessary. It is a crucial piece in the competition jigsaw puzzle. Besides advocating competition to government agencies, it defines the boundaries against anticompetitive conduct in the private sector, which may be driven towards such behavior if allowed to operate without any safeguards.

Within government proper, there is also the constant search for innovation and efficiency. The public sector service programme called PS21 is one example. The adoption of "best-sourcing" where internal service provisioning is subject to competitive comparison with outsourcing is another example and so is the pursuit of Public Private Partnerships.

Regulation is Necessary to Set the Boundary Conditions for Complex Systems

It is appropriate at this juncture to ask whether efficiency and the underlying free market principle are all there is to it in our economic development. The answer, especially in the light of the recent financial crisis and global recession, is that however attractive the principle of the free market, that principle alone cannot guarantee undiluted sustained economic growth.

The economic system as a complex adaptive system can never be free from sudden shocks. The nature of such complex systems is that they are capable of giving rise to sudden innovations and sudden shifts of the current equilibrium. Thus long periods of relative stability will be followed by sudden shifts or turbulence whether it be in technology or social change. In a similar fashion, the earth's crust stays quiescent ordinarily but can suddenly break out in severe earthquakes. This has given rise to the phrase "tectonic" change or "turbulence". Such sudden changes or shocks are not entirely bad because they often bring about innovation and needed adjustments that allow the system to reach a higher level of performance. This process can be equated to the "creative destruction" described by Joseph Schumpeter.

This behavior of complex systems therefore suggests the need for some regulation and constraints to be set for the system to operate within some reasonable limits. Setting those limits calls for considerable judgement. No doubt after the excesses of the banking system that led to the current crisis, there will be a move towards more regulation. There is however the threat of over-reaction and consequently the adoption of a regulatory regime that is excessive and curbs future innovation and change and in this way destroys its vitality over the long run.

The best policy intervention is one of defining the system at the boundaries and letting the so-called free market process operate to seek its own optimality subject to a judicious system of constraints. Choosing the appropriate constraints is an act of balance between stability and innovation. Thus our success in liberalization is complemented by our ability to put in place a regulatory regime that is able to prevent behaviors contrary to the public interest or result in market failure. Getting this balance right has enabled us to create an economic system that is highly efficient, competitive and somewhat resilient. Given our historical and geographic constraints, these qualities are essential to our future survival and prosperity.

CHAPTER 9

Inflation, Exchange Rate and the Singapore Economy: A Policy Simulation

CHOY KEEN MENG and TILAK ABEYSINGHE*

Introduction

Back in the 1970s, the world economy witnessed unprecedented and sustained increases in the prices of goods and services following the quadrupling of oil prices engineered by the Organization of the Petroleum Exporting Countries (OPEC) cartel. Annual inflation rates rose to double-digit figures in the industrialized nations, aggravated by the loose monetary policies of many governments. Economic historians subsequently called this event the Great Inflation. It took tough leaders with Monetarist leanings — Ronald Reagan in the US and Margaret Thatcher in the UK — and harsh economic recessions to finally rid their countries of the inflation scourge in the early 1980s.

* This paper was first presented at the Singapore Economic Policy Forum held in October 2008. We shall like to thank Gu Jiaying for excellent research assistance.

Now largely forgotten, memories of the Great Inflation were recently rekindled when the prices of primary commodities such as wheat, rice, soybean and oil more than doubled between 2007 and mid-2008. This time, it was a confluence of factors that led to inflation rearing its ugly head again. First, there has been increasing demand for agricultural commodities to feed and clothe the world's growing population and also to produce bio-fuels. Second, China has shown an insatiable appetite for energy and raw material imports to power her industrialization process. Third, urban creep and climate change has resulted in a limited supply of arable land while extraction costs for mineral resources have risen at the same time. Lastly, geopolitical developments and market speculation have contributed no small part to the sharp increases seen in both food and energy prices.

The key lessons learnt from the Great Inflation is that inflation should be tackled early and perhaps more important, second-round price effects originating from heightened inflationary expectations must not be allowed to take root and generate a wage-price spiral. These risks are now clearly recognized by central banks around the world, including the Monetary Authority of Singapore (MAS). Indeed, the MAS has presided over a historical inflation record that is the envy of the developed and developing worlds — an annual average of 1.4 percent over the last 25 years — by gradually appreciating the Singapore dollar exchange rate against the currencies of her major trading partners.

We examine in this chapter the impact of high commodity prices on the Singapore economy, which is heavily dependent on imported products and raw materials. And given the MAS's objective of keeping inflation low and stable, we analyze the effectiveness of a monetary policy designed to neutralize foreign price shocks. Finally, we quantify the economic costs of such an anti-inflation policy. The methodology used for all of these purposes is computer simulations of a large-scale macroeconometric model of the Singapore economy, which will be described next.

The ESU01 Model of the Singapore Economy

To trace out the repercussions of foreign inflation, we need a stylized account of the Singapore economy's workings. One such representation is provided by the ESU01 macroeconometric model.[1] In this section, we will explain the transmission mechanisms of external price shocks to domestic macroeconomic variables built into the model, as depicted schematically by the flowchart in Fig. 9.1.

The ESU01 model consists of 62 equations: 36 behavioral equations and 26 identities. Two behavioral equations, estimated on quarterly data from 1987 to 2003, are of vital importance in understanding the price transmission mechanism. The first is the equation for the prices of imported merchandise:

$$\Delta \ln P_t^m = -0.004 - 0.3\Delta \ln NEER_t - 0.05\Delta \ln NEER_{t-1} - 0.114\Delta \ln NEER_{t-2}$$
$$-0.018\Delta \ln NEER_{t-3} - 0.14\Delta \ln NEER_{t-4} + 1.29\Delta \ln P_t^f$$
$$-0.37\Delta \ln P_{t-1}^f + 0.388\Delta \ln P_{t-2}^f - 0.046\Delta \ln P_{t-3}^f - 0.166\Delta \ln P_{t-4}^f$$
$$+0.07\Delta P_t^{oil} + 0.02\Delta P_{t-1}^{oil} + 0.0016\Delta P_{t-2}^{oil} - 0.014\Delta P_{t-3}^{oil} + 0.015\Delta P_{t-4}^{oil}$$

where the logarithmic differencing operator ($\Delta \ln$) converts variables into approximate inflation rates. Fleshing out the upper left-hand corner of Fig. 9.1, the above regression says that import price inflation is a function of foreign producer prices (P^f) and the crude oil price (P^{oil}). However, the negative coefficients attached to the nominal effective exchange rate (NEER) suggest that a stronger Singapore dollar mitigates imported inflation by making foreign goods cheaper in the local currency. This exchange rate pass-through process, moreover, takes a year to be effected.

---

[1] Full details of the model are found in T. Abeysinghe and K.M. Choy (2007). *The Singapore Economy: An Econometric Perspective*. Routledge.

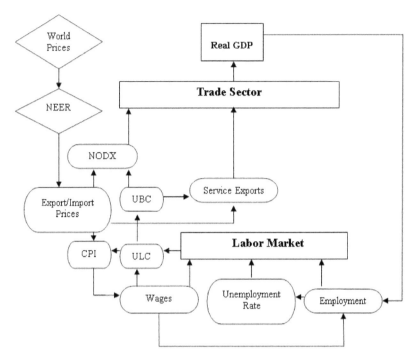

Fig. 9.1:   Transmission mechanisms of price shocks.

The second crucial relationship in the model forges a direct link between the import and consumer price indexes:

$$\Delta \ln CPI_t = 0.0007 + 0.48\Delta \ln CPI_{t-1} + 0.084\Delta \ln P_t^m$$
$$-0.071[\ln CPI - 0.45\ln P^m - 0.55\ln ULC^{NT}]_{t-1} + 0.0009GST_t.$$

This equation, specified in "error correction" form, states that consumer price inflation (CPI) depends largely on its own momentum and on the cost of imported goods (P^m) because they constitute a large proportion of the household's typical consumption bundle. In the long run, inflation is also caused by rising unit labor costs (ULC) of producing non-traded goods and services. This equation also shows a mild impact of the Goods and Services Tax (GST) on inflation.

In addition, it is also assumed that there is zero foreign currency pass-through of NEER changes to the prices of Singapore's exports, both merchandise and service.[2] Such an assumption is reasonable since Singapore is a textbook example of a price-taker in world markets on account of her small size and openness to trade.

Moving to the labor market at the bottom of Fig. 9.1, we see that an increase in consumer prices compels workers to demand higher nominal wages in an attempt to preserve the purchasing power of their earnings. This drives up unit labor costs of production as well as unit business costs (UBC), the latter including other non-wage operating expenses such as rentals and utilities. A higher ULC in turn generates a second-round increase in the CPI (see the equation above), which further reduces real disposable incomes and triggers a cutback in private consumption spending. But the story does not end here.

On the production side, the escalation of UBC erodes Singapore's economic competitiveness by raising the final prices of locally made goods and services. The all-important non-oil domestic exports (NODX) and service exports fall as a result. In other words, what started out as nominal price shocks have now made their impact felt on the real economy. With a retrenchment of output in the trade sector of the ESU01 model comes a concomitant decline in real gross domestic product (GDP) growth, as exports are the biggest contributor to the economy's aggregate demand. As aggregate demand slows, the demand for labor follows suit, leading to a fall in employment and a rise in the unemployment rate.

Scenarios

We now paint the economic scenarios for global price shocks and the central bank's response to them that will provide the backdrop

---

[2] An appreciation of the effective exchange rate, for example, will tend to lower the profit margins of exporters, even though it also reduces the prices of imported raw materials denominated in domestic currency.

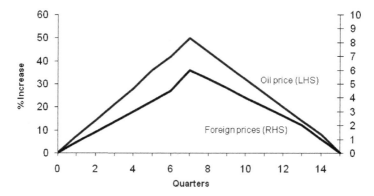

Fig. 9.2:   Foreign price shocks scenarios.

for the model-based simulations. Roughly speaking, the simulated scenarios mimic the pattern of commodity price increases seen in 2007 and 2008, albeit not their exact magnitudes and timing. In particular, prices are envisaged to increase steadily for about two years before retreating in the inverted V shape shown in Fig. 9.2.

With higher commodity prices, the foreign price index rises by an average of 0.9 percent per quarter for seven quarters until it peaks at six percent above the initial level. Then it commences a gradual decline which eventually brings world producer prices back to the starting point. In contrast, the spot oil price spikes up by 7.1 percent every quarter until prices are 50 percent higher at the zenith. Thereafter, the oil price shock fades away and finally dissipates.

From the import price equation, we can work out the appreciation of the NEER required for the external price shocks to be fully offset and not have an impact on import costs. The implied policy path for the exchange rate is plotted in Fig. 9.3 and not surprisingly, it resembles the pattern of the price shocks. Simulating the ESU01 model under this currency appreciation scenario will tell us whether monetary policy in Singapore can be used effectively to counteract increases in global commodity and energy prices, and what its side-effects on the macroeconomy are.

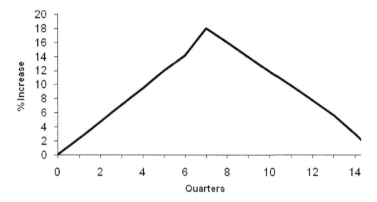

Fig. 9.3:   Monetary policy scenario: NEER appreciation.

The simulation methodology itself involves the following steps:

1. First solve for the equilibrium values of the macroeconomic variables in the ESU01 model in the absence of price shocks (the "control" solution).[3]
2. Subject the model to the foreign shocks described above and recompute the equilibrium profiles of variables (the "shock" scenario).
3. Add the monetary policy reaction to the price shocks and solve the model again (the "offset" scenario).

In the simulation results that follow, we report the percentage (or percentage point as the case may be) deviations of macroeconomic indicators in the shock and offset solutions from their control values, and interpret these numbers as quantifying the effects on the Singapore economy of the commodity price increases and monetary policy intervention respectively.

---

[3] This is typically done using a dedicated statistics or econometrics software such as EViews in the case of the ESU01 model.

Simulation Results

The results of the simulation experiments are graphed in Figs. 9.4 and 9.5 and reported numerically in Table 9.1. In each plot, the darker line represents the outcome under the shock scenario and

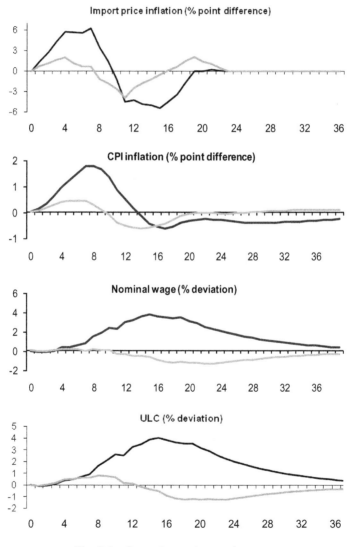

Fig. 9.4:   Impact on prices and wages.

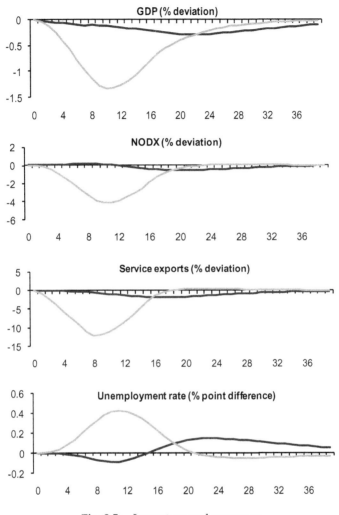

Fig. 9.5:   Impact on real economy.

the lighter line, the offset scenario. The horizontal axis measures time passed, in quarters, since the onset of the price shocks.

Starting with the top plot in Fig. 9.4, one can see that without a NEER appreciation, commodity shocks are directly translated into import prices in the first instance, with their rate of increase peaking at 6.2 percent in the seventh quarter. The inflation rate

Table 9.1: Simulation results from ESU01 model.

Variable	Scenario	Time (quarters)				
		1	4	8	12	36
Import inflation	Shock	1.4	5.8	3.4	−4.3	0.0
	Offset	0.7	2.0	−1.2	−2.4	0.0
CPI inflation	Shock	0.1	1.0	1.8	0.5	−0.3
	Offset	0.1	0.4	0.3	−0.5	0.1
Nominal wage	Shock	−0.1	0.3	1.5	2.9	0.5
	Offset	−0.1	0.1	0.1	−0.3	−0.4
ULC	Shock	−0.1	0.4	1.7	3.2	0.4
	Offset	0.0	0.5	0.8	0.1	−0.3
Real GDP	Shock	0.0	−0.1	−0.1	−0.2	−0.1
	Offset	0.0	−0.4	−1.2	−1.3	0.0
NODX	Shock	0.0	0.1	0.1	−0.1	−0.1
	Offset	0.0	−0.9	−3.3	−3.9	0.1
Service exports	Shock	0.0	−0.1	−0.5	−1.2	−0.3
	Offset	−0.7	−5.6	−12.2	−8.4	0.2
Unemployment	Shock	0.0	0.0	−0.1	−0.1	0.0
	Offset	0.0	0.1	0.3	0.4	0.0

Note: Figures are percentage deviations from the control solution except for inflation and unemployment rates, which are percentage point deviations.

then comes down as the shocks subside and it undershoots the long-run equilibrium before stabilizing after five years. This transmission pattern is inherited by CPI inflation, although the latter's increases are smoother and slightly delayed. Two years after the foreign price disturbances hit Singapore, average consumer prices have risen by 1.8 percentage points, compared to a scenario where there are no shocks.

The last two charts in Fig. 9.4 describe the secondary effects on the labor market of the commodity and oil price increases. During the first year, wages and costs do not react as yet to higher import and consumer prices. After that, however, rising inflation rates begin to feed demands for wage increases on the part of unions and workers. Consequently, the nominal wage rate and ULC increase by four percent in the subsequent years.

Since inflation rises much earlier than wages, household real incomes are eroded, thus hurting consumer spending and, via an accelerator-like effect, business investment too. Real GDP growth begins to slip (Fig. 9.5). Furthermore, the postulated effects of inflated business costs on export performance are borne out by the computer simulations: there is a small decline in NODX and a more significant fall in service exports of 1.2 percent after three years, exacerbating the slowdown in economic growth and raising the unemployment rate marginally.

The experimental results are very different when the exchange rate is allowed to appreciate under the alternative offset scenario. Import costs increase by two percent at most in Fig. 9.4, suggesting that monetary policy is effective in subduing external price pressures. As a consequence, the CPI rises by only half a percentage point. The action takes place elsewhere instead — on the real economic front in Fig. 9.5. There, the hump-shaped declines recorded for real GDP, NODX and service exports bear testimony to the adverse impact that a stronger exchange rate has on Singapore's ability to compete in international markets and they also suggest that exchange rate policy works with long and variable lags.

At their nadir, non-oil exports tumble by about four percent while service trade earnings, which deteriorate at a faster pace, drop by three times that amount. This explains why aggregate output declines by up to 1.3 percent compared with the control outcome and pushes the unemployment rate higher by 0.4 of a percentage point. The last finding implies an empirical Okun's Law[4] for Singapore: a one percentage point increase in unemployment is associated with a 3.2 percent drop in the ratio of GDP to full capacity output.

In summary, the monetary policy simulation of the ESU01 model has shown that an attempt by the MAS to fully offset foreign price shocks will lead to a period of increased unemployment and reduced output. Despite its anti-inflation credentials, this puts the

---

[4] Named after the economist Arthur M. Okun, who was the chairman of the US Council of Economic Advisors between 1968 and 1969.

central bank in a bind because it has now to weigh the benefits of stabilizing prices against the costs of slowing growth. We will not discuss the normative issues involved, but it is evident that the resolution of this policy dilemma will be greatly aided by an estimate of the output cost of disinflation.

A one-number summary of this cost also suggested by Arthur Okun is the "sacrifice ratio", defined as the cumulative loss in output entailed by a one percentage point reduction in inflation. Figure 9.6 illustrates the conventional measurement of the sacrifice ratio. The output loss resulting from a one percentage point decline in the inflation rate in the lower diagram is equal to the shaded area bounded by the actual path of real GDP under the disinflation policy and its long-term trend in the upper diagram. In terms of our simulation results, the sacrifice ratio can be calculated as:

$$\text{Sacrifice ratio} = \frac{\sum_{t=1}^{36}\left(GDP_t^{\text{shock}} - GDP_t^{\text{offset}}\right)}{\sum_{t=1}^{36}\left(\Delta CPI_t^{\text{shock}} - \Delta CPI_t^{\text{offset}}\right)}$$

or the further reduction in real output that occurs over 36 quarters under the offset scenario divided by the corresponding decrease in the consumer inflation rate, both *vis-à-vis* the pure price shock scenario. The ESU01 model simulations reveal that the sacrifice ratio for Singapore is around 2, compared to about 3–4 for the US and an average of 2.5 for the OECD countries. In other words, to bring inflation down by a full percentage point, real GDP growth has to be lowered by two percent.

Conclusions

In this chapter, we have demonstrated through computer simulations of a large macroeconometric model of the Singapore economy that world commodity price increases similar to those witnessed recently will be quickly transmitted into higher domestic inflation rates in the absence of monetary policy tightening. In principle, imported inflation can be almost fully countered with

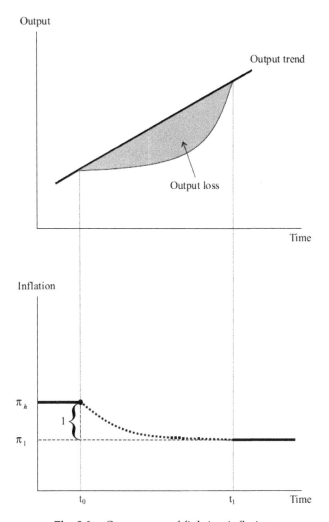

Fig. 9.6: Output cost of fighting inflation.

(Diagram taken from A.J. Filardo, "New Evidence on the Output Cost of Fighting Inflation", *Federal Reserve Bank of Kansas City Economic Review*, Third Quarter 1998).

a sustained appreciation of the Singapore dollar effective exchange rate. However, this will entail a significant slowdown in real GDP growth. To wit, a one percentage point reduction in CPI inflation requires the nation to forego two percent of output.

In reality, the MAS appears to have opted for a partial offset of foreign price shocks beginning with the quicker appreciation of the NEER in October 2007. This monetary policy response has been supplemented by fiscal support schemes to cushion the most vulnerable in society from the effects of price increases. Such a policy mix has considerable merit as it alleviates the worst effects of the inflation scourge without, at the same time, exacting an unduly large cost on economic growth.

CHAPTER 10

Workfare, Not Welfare: An Exploration on International Experiences and Policy Implications for Singapore

KAMPON ADIREKSOMBAT

The In-Work Benefit (IWB) program improves in-work benefits relative to out-of-work benefit and hence increases incentives to work. The policy was firstly adopted by the UK in 1971, then by the US in 1975. With the success of the In-Work-Benefit programs in the UK and the US, the programs have been disseminated across countries. In 2008, the IWB programs have been adopted by 12 countries, namely the United Kingdom, the United States, Canada, Ireland, New Zealand, Finland, Belgium, France, Netherlands, Denmark, Austria, and Singapore. All of them are the OECD countries with the exception of Singapore. More countries are considering adoption of the program. Israel did a pilot basis in 2008. In South Korea, the earned income tax credit will commence payment from 2009. The IMF recommended that countries in Eastern Europe, such as Czech Republic and

Slovenia, consider In-Work-Benefit programs to mitigate income inequality in their countries.

History of In-Work Benefit (IWB) Programs

The In-Work-Benefit programs are also called employment-conditional programs. These benefits are paid only to a low-income person in a part-time or full-time job, and therefore the programs also improve income distribution.

Table 10.1 provides a summary of the main features of the currently existing In-Work Benefit programs in 12 countries. Countries are ordered by the year of introduction of the first in-work-benefit program respectively. In some countries, the current program may not have the same name as when first introduced. For example, the UK in-work-benefit program was called the Family Income Supplement (FIS) when it was introduced in 1971, but now called the Working Tax Credit (WTC).

Due to different national institutions and policy goals, there is variation in the main features of the programs adopted by these countries. For example, while the Earned Income Tax Credit (EITC) in the US aims at reducing poverty, the Employed Person's Tax Credit (EPTC) in Netherlands aims to tackle the problem of unemployment among low-income people. As a result, the EPTC eligibility is based on individual income. Focusing on the effects in labor force participation, there are two major features across countries worth discussing, namely unit of assessment and whether the benefit is refundable.

The effects of benefits on labor supply may vary by the unit of assessment whether it depends on individual or family income. If the benefits vary by family income, this may cause an adverse effect of a decrease in the incentive to work for the spouse (Dickert, Houser and Scholz, 1995; Eissa and Hoynes, 2004; Stancanelli, 2008).

Another feature of the program that may have significant effect on the labor supply is whether the benefit is refundable. If the

Table 10.1: In-work benefit program adoption.

Country	Current Program	Year of Introduction	Unit of Assessment	Refundable
UK	Working Tax Credit	1971	Families	Yes
US	Earned Income Tax Credit	1975	Families	Yes
Canada	Working Income Tax Benefit	1978	Families	Yes
Ireland	Family Income Supplement	1984	Families	Yes
New Zealand	Working for Families Tax Credits	1986	Families	Yes
Finland	Earned Income Allowance	1996	Individual	No
Belgium	Earned Income Tax Credit	2001	Individual	Yes
France	Prime Pour l'Empoli	2001	Families	Yes
Netherlands	Employed Person's Tax Credit	2001	Individual	No
Denmark	Earned Income Tax Credit	2003	Individual	No
Austria	Sole Earner (Single Parent) Tax Credit	2005	Families	Yes
Singapore	Workfare Income Supplement	2007	Individual	Yes

Sources: Gradus and Justling (2001); Person and Scarpetta (2000); Duncan and Greenaway (2004); OECD (Social Policy Division — Directorate of Employment, Labour and Social Affairs, Country Chapter, 2004); Banks *et al.* (2005); International Monetary Fund (Country Report No. 04/236, 2004 and 08/62, 2008); Ministry of Finance, Singapore (Budget Statement, 2007).

benefits are refundable, the programs are more relevant to low-income workers because most of them did not have to pay tax in the first place. The effects of non-refundable benefits are limited. For example, in Finland, unlike the refundable tax credits, the effect of the Earned Income Allowance is the product of the deduction and the marginal tax rate.

Moreover, there are several features that vary across countries. For example, in the UK, the benefits are conditional upon a minimum number of hours of work, while in the US, the benefits are not time-limited, but depend on household income. The generosity of benefits and eligibility criteria also vary substantially across countries, depending on other components of redistribution policy and institutional features of the social welfare system, for example, out-of-work benefits and minimum wage policies.

The IWB Structure

The benefits of the In-Work-Benefit programs in most of the adopted countries share similar structures. While the in-work benefit programs are called by various names, it will be called "Earned Income Tax Credit" or EITC, as in the US, from hereon. The EITC will also be used as an example to examine the structure of the IWB program. Fig. 10.1 presents the EITC structures during the 1990s. The EITC benefit equals a specified percentage of earned income up to a maximum dollar amount over the "phase-in range". Taxpayers receive the maximum credit over a range of income termed the "flat range". The credit then diminishes to zero over the "phase-out range". The credit rates and maximum credits also vary with the number of children in the household. For example, in 1998, the maximum credit for a family with one child was US$2271, while that for a family with two or more children was US$3756. The EITC is refundable and claimants are paid regardless of whether the credit-qualified taxpayer has any federal income tax liability. The EITC payment is typically made once a year as an adjustment to tax liabilities or refunds. For those who have children and want to claim the EITC, their children need to pass an age, relationship, and residence test to qualify. For example, the age test in 2000 requires the qualifying child to be under 19 years old or under 24 years old if she/he is a full-time student, or any age if she/he is completely disabled. The relationship test requires the claimant to be the parent or the grandparent of the qualifying child.

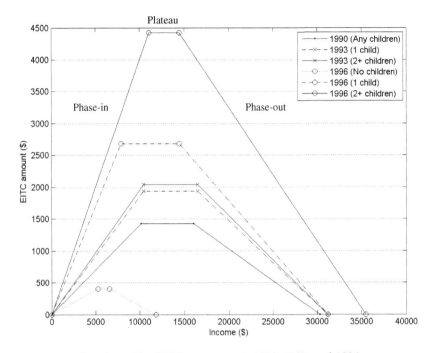

Fig. 10.1:   The EITC structures in 1990, 1993, and 1996.

Source: Author's calculations from the House Ways and Means Committee Green Book (2004).

Labor Supply Response to the EITC

A. Theoretical Predictions

From the static labor-leisure model, the EITC expansion affects the intensive and extensive margins of the labor supply of unmarried women. For a non-worker who was out of the labor force before the expansion, the static labor-leisure model predicts that the EITC expansion will expand her budget set when she enters the labor force. With no earned income before the expansion, there will be only a positive substitution effect but no income effect due to an increase in the effective wage (marginal value of working). As a result, some will choose to participate in the labor force.

For a worker who was already in the labor force, the effect of the expansion on her hours of work is ambiguous, depending on the range of EITC in which her income falls before and after the expansion. If her income falls in the "phase-in range", in theory, there will be a positive substitution effect and a negative income effect, assuming that leisure is a "normal good". Thus, the net effect is ambiguous. If her income falls in the "flat range", there is only a negative income effect; consequently, the expansion leads to a decrease in hours of work. If her income falls in the "phase-out range", a diminishing credit implies a lower effective wage relative to the absence of the EITC. This negative substitution effect results in a reduction in hours of work, as does the negative income effect. Finally, if her income was beyond the credit region, she may decide to reduce her hours of work to be eligible for the credit.

B. Empirical Evidence

With mixed effects on individual decisions to work, a number of micro-level studies support In-Work-Benefit policies as an effective employment policy (Holt and Scholz, 2003, for a summary of the EITC and labor supply in the US; Brewer and Browne, 2006, for the UK; Ochel, 2001, for Ireland; Nellissen, Fontein and Soest, 2005, for the Netherlands; Stancanelli, 2008, for France). For example, existing research suggests that the EITC expansion substantially increased the labor supply of American unmarried women, but decreased the labor supply of married women (Dickert *et al.*, 1995). Among unmarried women, recent studies also find that those with two or more children substantially increased their labor force participation as compared to those with no children and those with one child due to differential increases in the maximum credits in 1993 that favored the two- or more-children group (Hotz *et al.*, 2006; Adireksombat, 2009a).

Effective Anti-Poverty Instrument

By its structure, the IWB is limited to low-income individuals or families. In the US, over 60 percent of EITC payments go to taxpayers with pre-EITC incomes below the poverty line and approximately half of total payments directly reduce the poverty gap (Scholz and Levine, 2000). In 1997 and 1998, EITC removed 4.3 million persons from poverty in the US (Council of Economic Advisors, 1998, 2000). More recent studies also support the policies as an effective anti-poverty instrument (Neumark and Wascher, 2001; Adireksombat, 2009b).

The programs are effectively reaching the targeted groups. Several EITC utilization studies suggest that more than three-quarters of eligible households claim the credit (Scholz, 1994; the General Accounting Office, 2001). In the UK, the WFTC take up rates are 87 percent for lone parents and 62 percent for couples (Brewer *et al.*, 2005). In Ireland, the early years of the program, the take-up rate was only 30 percent, but the Irish government has undertaken several campaigns to raise awareness of the in-work-benefit programs (Stephens, 2005). In France, over 14 percent of the total population had received the credits in 2005. In conclusion, the take-up rates are very high in the US and UK. For other users, the rate is increasing.

Another upside of the programs is low administration and compliance costs. Most of the countries with In-Work-Benefit program use their tax administrator to operate the programs, for example, the IRS in the US, resulting in low tax compliance and administration costs because tax payers and tax administrator could save time and money to claim and pay the benefits. However, the programs are costly. In the US, the EITC costs more than US$43 billion (U.S. Office of Management and Budget, 2008).

Workfare Income Supplement (WIS) Scheme

In 2007, the Singapore Government restructured the Central Provident Fund (CPF) for low-income workers. To complement the CPF changes, Workfare Income Supplement, the Singaporean IWB, was also introduced in the same year. The main purpose of the scheme is to increase the take-home pay and CPF savings of low-income workers.

The target group of WIS scheme is workers (with Singapore citizenship) aged 35 years and above. To be eligible for the benefit, the worker has to work at least three months in any six-month period in the calendar year, or at least six months in the calendar year. They also must earn an average monthly income above $50 and up to $1500 and stay in a property with an annual value of not more than $10,000 as at the end of the year. Approximately, the WIS scheme cost is $400 million and 438,000 Singaporean workers are expected to receive the payment. The WIS is intended to be a permanent scheme in the social safety system. However, as of February 2009, the WIS is on pilot basis and expected to be reviewed in 2010.

The WIS payments vary with age, monthly income, number of working months, and whether the worker is a formal employee (with CPF) or a self-employed person. Figure 10.2 presents the WIS maximum payments by age groups in 2008. The maximum payments are higher for older workers. The maximum payment for workers between the ages of 35 and 45 is $900, the ages of 45 and 55 is $1,200, the ages of 55 and 65 is $1,800, and aged above 65 is $2,400.

For the formal employee, the WIS payment is split into Cash and CPF according to the ratio 1 to 2.5. For example, a worker who

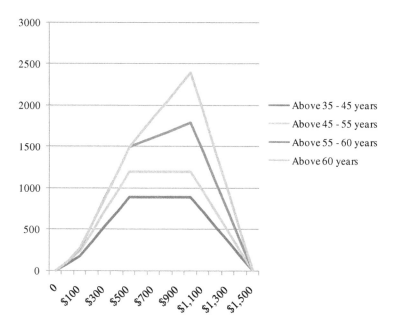

Fig. 10.2:   WIS maximum payments by age groups in 2008.

is eligible for a $900 benefit will receive $258 in cash and $642 in her CPF account. The payment also varies with the number of working months during the year. While those who work for at least six months in the calendar year will receive the full amount of the payment, those who work three months in any six-month period in that calendar year will receive only half of the payment. As self-employed and informal workers contribute much less to the CPF, their WIS payments will be two-thirds of the amount for employees. And the WIS will be paid entirely into their Medisave accounts.

The WIS payments are made twice a year. The first payment is for work done from January to June and the second payment is for work done for the whole year. Those who have worked for at least three months in the first half of the year will be eligible for the first payment, which will be up to 50 percent of the full Workfare payment based on their age and average monthly income. In 2008, workers received their payments in January and April, based on their 2007 income.[1] The CPF board automatically verifies workers' employment income and pay WIS to their CPF account. Workers will be notified via mail before the payment will be made. Moreover, WIS payments are not taxable.

Using WIS as an instrument to mitigate the effects of the global financial crisis, in 2009 the government budget temporally provided additional 50 percent of the usual WIS payments that low-income workers would receive over the period of 2009. This additional payment is fully in cash. To increase the size of the target group, the 2009 budget also relaxed the work eligibility criteria of the WIS Special Payment to allow workers with less regular employment to also qualify for the scheme.

Prediction for Labor Supply Response to the WIS

Figures 10.1 and 10.2 show that the EITC and WIS share very similar structures. In theory, we could expect that these two IWB

---

[1] Self-employed and informal workers received WIS payments after formal workers. In 2008 they received the payments in January and May.

programs should also share the positive effects on labor supply. While the EITC benefit varies with a family income, the WIS benefit varies with an individual income. As a result, WIS should not lead to an adverse effect of a decrease in the incentive to work for the spouse as in case of the EITC. With higher amount of maximum credits, in theory, after 2007 those who are older should help to increase the labor supply, all else being equal. Moreover, we should expect that the WIS would be an effective anti-poverty instrument as the EITC is. However, compared to the EITC, which also provides the credit to resident aliens, WIS is available only to Singaporean workers; as a result, the potential positive effects on labor supply might be attenuated.

As discussed earlier, previous studies in several countries suggests that the IWB programs lead to an increase in labor supply. The question of whether the IWB will be effective in Singapore is to be answered by future empirical research. One potential empirical strategy is to use the reduced-form model which is commonly referred to as the natural experiment or the Difference-in-Difference (DID) approach. The advantage of the DID approach is simplicity and transparency in the assumptions that allow the identification of key parameters. Unlike a true experiment, in which treatment and comparison groups are randomly chosen, the treatment (affected) and comparison groups (not affected) in natural experiments arise from the particular policy change. Therefore, to control systematic differences between the control and treatment groups, two periods of data (before and after the policy change) are needed. Other exogenous variables could also be included in the regression equation to control for the fact that the populations sampled may differ systematically over the two periods.

For example, we could empirically examine the effect of WIS on labor force participation by using a DID approach with a control group of working adults aged 25–35 (not eligible for WIS) and four treatment groups of those who are 35–45, 45–55, 55–60 and above 60 (WIS target groups). The DID estimates compare changes of the labor force participation before and after 2007 between the treatment groups and the comparison group. To achieve unbiased estimate of the WIS effect, in the empirical model, we could also include other policy and demographic variables, such as a dummy for Jobs Credit scheme and other sources of income, to control for other factors that could also affect the labor supply of WIS workers.

Suggestion

Compared to the American experience, the EITC provided a fixed amount of credit since 1975 when the EITC was introduced. The EITC payments were eroded by inflation until the EITC expansion in 1986 increased the maximum credit to have a real value equal to that of the credit in 1975, and indexed the EITC value for inflation. To make up for the loss in the value of the WIS payments for workers due to inflation, the Singapore government might want to index the payment for inflation. This will also save the government spending on the scheme due to an increase in the income threshold.

References

Adireksombat, K. (2009a). The Effect of the 1993 Earned Income Tax Credit Expansion on the Labor Supply of Unmarried Women. Unpublished Manuscript, Nanyang Technological University.

Adireksombat, K. (2009b). The Incidence of the Earned Income Tax Credit. Unpublished Manuscript, Nanyang Technological University.

Banks, J., R. Disney, A. Duncan and J. V. Reenen (2005). The Internationalisation of Public Welfare Policy. *Economic Journal*, 115, C62–C81.

Brewer, M. and J. Browne (2006). The Effect of the Working Families' Tax Credit on Labour Market Participation. Institute for Fiscal Studies Briefing Note No. 69.

Brewer, M., A. Duncan, A. Shephard and M. J. Suarez (2005). Did Working Families' Tax Credit Work? The Impact of In-Work Support on Labour Supply in Great Britain. CPE Working Paper 4/05.

Dickert, S., S. Houser and J. K. Scholz (1995). The Earned Income Tax Credit and Transfer Programs: A Study of Labor Market and Program Participation. In *Tax Policy and the Economy*, Poterba, J. M. (ed.), Cambridge: MIT Press, pp. 1–50.

Duncan, A. and D. Greenaway (2004). *Tax Credits and Welfare for Working Families: A Case of UK-US Policy Transfer.* Amsterdam: Elsevier.

Eissa, N. and W. H. Hilary (2004). Taxes and the Labor Market Participation of Married Couples: The Earned Income Tax Credit. *Journal of Public Economics*, 88, pp. 1931–1958.

Gradus, R. H. J. M. and J. M. Julsing (2001). Comparing Different European Income Tax Policies Making Work Pay. OCFEB Research Memorundum 0101.

Hotz, V. J. and J. K. Scholz (2003). The Earned Income Tax Credit. In *Means-Tested Transfer Programs in the United States*, Moffitt, R. (ed.), Chicago: University of Chicago Press and National Bureau of Economic Research.

Hotz, J. V., C. H. Mullin and J. K. Scholz (2006). Examining the Effect of the Earned Income Tax Credit on the Labor Market Participation of Families on Welfare. NBER Working Paper No. 11968.

Nelissen, J. H. M., P. F. Fontein and A. H. O. V. Soest (2005). *The Impact of Various Policy Measures on Employment in the Netherlands.* Centers of Applied Research.

Neumark, D. and W. Wascher (2001). Using the EITC to Help Poor Families: New Evidence and a Comparison with the Minimum Wage. *National Tax Journal*, pp. 281–318

OECD (2003). Making Work Pay Making Work Possible. In *OECD Employment Outlook* 2003.

Orchel, W. (2001). Financial Incentives to Work-Conceptions and Results in Great Britain, Ireland, and Canada. CESifo Working Paper No. 627.

Scholz, J. K. (1994). The Earned Income Tax Credit: Participation, Compliance, and Anti-poverty Effectiveness. *National Tax Journal*, 47, pp. 59–81

Scholz, J. K. and K. Levine (2000). The Evolution of Income Support Policy. Mimeograph, University of Wisconsin–Madison.

Stancanelli, E. G. F. (2008). Evaluating the Impact of the French Tax Credit on the Employment Rate of Women. *Journal of Public Economics*, 92, pp. 2036–2047.

Stephens, R. (2005). *Universal or Targeted: A Comparison of Poverty Programmes in Ireland and New Zealand*. Trinity College: The Policy Institute.

CHAPTER 11

What is Human Life Worth?

EUSTON QUAH, CHIA WAI–MUN and SNG HUI YING*

T he thought of putting a dollar value to a human life may provoke moral outrage but the process is necessary for good public policy. No country has an infinite amount of money and resources to spend on protecting and extending each citizen's life. At some point, choices have to be made in areas such as health-care and safety regulation. The value of a statistical life reflects what people are willing to spend to reduce small risks of death. It is a measure used widely to evaluate public policies in medicine, environmental regulation and transportation safety. A study was carried out in 2007 to determine the value of a statistical life in Singapore. 800 respondents were asked how much they were willing to pay to reduce small risks of death. From the study, it is estimated that the value of a statistical life in Singapore is between S$850,000 (US$615,950) and S$2.05 million (US$1.49 million). The value was close to that of South Korea and Taiwan but was lower than America's and Australia's.

* The authors are grateful to Lim Khee–Meng, Hoon Shi, Cheng Tianyin for their excellent research assistance. The authors also thank Alan Krupnick and Maureen Cropper for their helpful comments and advice.

Introduction

It is always distasteful to place a value on saving a human life. To many of us, human life is precious. Indeed, how can the value of a life even be calculated? For many people, they would give up all their wealth to avoid the loss of their own life. So, there is basically no upper limit on the value of life. If putting a price tag on life is a matter of great controversy, then why are we doing this? Although some may consider it morally wrong to even raise the question of the dollar value of life, in the real world, we are finding policymakers, jurors, health services researchers, academics and even private citizens attempting to determine how much a life is worth.

It is certainly easy to provoke moral outrage by suggesting that the policymakers are putting a dollar value on a life. However, despite its prima facie callousness, determining the value of a human life is necessary for good public policies. This is because society, with limited resources, cannot afford to spend an infinite amount of money and resources to protect and extend each person's life. It is simply too expensive to try to make everything perfectly safe. At some points, choices have to be made in the realm of health and safety regulation. Policymakers who have to obtain the greatest benefit for each dollar spent are often asked to decide on the extent in which they are willing to allocate resources to prevent unnecessary death rather than say improve education or ensure cleaner environment. When government agencies put a value on human life, it allows them to weigh the costs versus the lifesaving benefits of a proposed regulation. When government agencies use a lower figure for the value of life, then the less a life is worth to the government, the less the need for a safety regulation, such as stringent airline safety and tighter restrictions on pollution. To policy makers, the economic value of life is neither the total of one's income-earning potential nor the worth of a life. The value of a statistical life reflects what people are willing to spend to reduce small risks of death. It is a measure that is widely used for the evaluation of public policies in medicine, environment and transportation safety.

Different Approaches to Value a Statistical Life

Human life is precious. Yet at the same time, everyone takes risks as everyday life entails certain risks which can never be reduced to zero. Some of which, however, can be avoided by the expense of either time or money. When one pays to avoid potentially fatal risks, or accepts wealth in return to take such risks, the person is implicitly defining a trade-off between wealth and the probability of death. The ratio of the wealth one person is willing to accept (WTA) in exchange for a small increase in the probability of death or the ratio of the wealth one person is willing to pay (WTP) in exchange for a small decrease in the probability of death is expressed in units of dollars per death or is commonly known as value of a statistical life. This value does not reflect the value of an individual life, but is entirely based on the amount of money one person is willing to trade-off for a small change in his or her own risk. Literature survey found in Viscusi (1993) represents the best starting point for a value of statistical life estimates. Although researchers generally acknowledge that there are some formidable difficulties and challenges in measuring risk-dollar trade-offs, hundreds of analyses are found using widely varying methodologies to determine this value. Despite their differences, most of the studies center on one basic idea: the value of a statistical life should roughly correspond to the value that people place on their lives in their private decisions. Some of the most common methods developed are (1) *wage-risk analysis* which analyzes compensating wage differentials associated with risky jobs, (2) *averting behavior analysis* which examines risk-avoidance behavior in inherently risky situation, and (3) *contingent valuation surveys* which probe how much people are willing to pay for a small change in the risk of death.

Wage-risk analysis examines compensating wage differential associated with risky jobs. Two jobs can be different in a number of ways: one can be in a better city, or it can be in a more pleasant working environment, or it offers better fringe benefits, or it provides better future occupational advancement or it can be safer. In wage-risk analysis, economists estimate value of a statistical life by exploiting the difference in pay which stems from the difference in the risk of death. Consider the market for risky jobs. Suppose that, on average, workers face a death risk of 1 in 10,000 of being killed each year and that they are willing to accept this risk in return for an additional $200 in annual wage compensation. The value of a statistical life is consequently $2 million.

Averting behavior analysis examines risk-avoidance behavior in inherently risky situations. In this analysis the value of a statistical life is inferred from our product choices. Take for instance, airbag reduces the risk of death by 1 in 10,000 and if we can say for certain that we will buy a car with airbags at the costs of $200, then we can infer that we are placing an implicit valuation on our life to be at least $2 million.

Contingent valuation analysis probes directly how much people are willing to pay or accept for a small change in the risk of death. In this analysis, a number of people are asked the amount of money he or she is willing to pay to reduce the risk of death by 1 in 10,000. The question might be whether the person would pay $100 to lower the risk of death and so on until the person says he would refuse to pay further. Suppose the person stops at $200 for a 1 in 10,000 risk reduction. The value of a statistical life is again $2 million.

In all these analyses, $2 million is the value of a statistical life. This number, however, does not imply that people would accept death if paid $2 million or that they could come up with $2 million to buy out a certain death. Rather, it captures only the amount at which people are willing to trade-off for a small change in the risk of death. Additionally, this value reflects only the value of a typical life, without any personal information attached. There is no reason indeed to expect that the value of a statistical life would equal the value of an identified life. However, it is possible to conjecture which one is larger.

Benefit Transfer

Estimating the value of a statistical life can be time-consuming and costly. Therefore, it has been a common practice to use a benefit transfer approach to transfer such values with adjustments for income differential across countries i.e., from countries where these values have been made available, usually based on the US or European studies, to countries where these values have not been estimated. Generally, the transferred value is scaled by the ratio of per capita income of the country in which such value does not exist to the per capita income of the country of which the value is adapted to correct for the income differential between the two countries. Then, the adapted value is adjusted using the elasticity of willingness-to-pay with respect to income which measures the responsiveness of willingness-to-pay for a small percentage change in income. While the income elasticity should be positive on theoretical grounds, estimating values of a statistical life across countries using the benefit transfer approach requires empirical estimates of this elasticity. Within individual countries, the elasticity of willingness-to-pay with respect to income has been empirically documented. Viscusi and Evans (1990) find that the willingness-to-pay varies linearly with income in the US. A study by Jones–Lee *et al.* (1987) estimates the income elasticity to be between 0.3 and 0.6 in UK. A study conducted by Alberini and Krupnick (1998) finds the income elasticity of about 0.32 in Taiwan while another study by Loehman *et al.* (1979) estimates that the income elasticity is between 0.26 to 0.6.

In estimating the value of a statistical life in Singapore, we first scale the transferred unit economic values by the ratio of per capita income of Singapore to the per capita income of the developed country from which these values are adapted so that income differential between the two countries can be corrected. Then, we adjust the adapted values using the elasticity of willingness-to-pay with respect to income. For the case of estimating the value of a statistical life in Singapore, we use the value of a statistical life in the United Kingdom. The adjustment is done based on the Purchasing Power Parity estimates of Gross Domestic Product

(*GDP*) per capita of Singapore and the United Kingdom. The value of a statistical life of Singapore is computed based on the following expression:

$$VSL_{\text{Sing}}^{07} = VSL_{\text{UK}}^{07} \times \left(\frac{GDP_{\text{Sing}}^{07}}{GDP_{\text{UK}}^{07}} \right)^{e} \qquad (1)$$

where VSL_{Sing}^{07} is the value of a statistical life for Singapore in 2007, VSL_{UK}^{07} is the value of a statistical life for the UK in 2007 prices, GDP_{Sing}^{07} is the GDP of Singapore in 2007, GDP_{UK}^{07} is the GDP of the UK in 2007 and e is the elasticity of willingness-to-pay with respect to income. VSL_{UK}^{07} = US\$2.378 million. From the World Development Indicator Online, GDP_{UK}^{07} and GDP_{Sing}^{07} are US\$33,717 and US\$46,939, respectively. Following Alberini and Krupnick (1998) we take $e = 0.32$. Thus, for the estimation of the value of a statistical life for Singapore, the income elasticity of willingness-to-pay is taken to be equal to that of Taiwan. This is because the economic conditions of Singapore and Taiwan are largely similar. Quah and Boon (2003) also use 0.32 as the income elasticity of willingness-to-pay. Since $(GDP_{\text{Sing}}^{07} / GDP_{\text{UK}}^{07})$ = US\$46,939/US\$33,717 = 1.39, VSL_{Sing}^{07} = US\$2.378 million $\times 1.39^{0.32}$ = US\$2.6425 million which is approximately S\$3.6465 million.

Indigenous Value of a Statistical Life in Singapore

The benefit transfer approach, even though being widely used, seems to introduce some unique issues and challenges making this practice subject to controversy and scrutiny. These issues include how to convert values from one currency to another, how to account for differences in quantifiable characteristics between countries such as income, and how to account for differences in non-quantifiable characteristics such as cultural differences (Ready and Navrud, 2006).

Only very few countries have developed studies estimating value of a statistical life. While the bulk of studies have been conducted in many developed countries, particularly the United States and Western Europe, no such study has been conducted in Singapore. Motivated by the lack of indigenous estimates of the value of a statistical life which in turn provides a reference point for assessing public policies which ultimately involve a balancing of additional risk of death reduction and the incremental costs, we elicited Singaporeans' willingness-to-pay for the risk of mortality reduction using a contingent valuation survey. Results obtained from the survey were used to derive the value of a statistical life for Singapore. The value of a statistical life was estimated by asking how much Singaporeans and her permanent residents are willing to pay for a small reduction in the probability that they would die.

A target population of age 40 and above was chosen because the present demographic structure suggests that more than 55 percent of the population are aged 40 to 75, and this more elderly population tends to benefit disproportionately from health and environmental programs. We asked people how much they are willing to pay for an abstract private good that will reduce their risk of dying, over a 10-year interval, by 5 in 10,000 and 1 in 10,000, respectively. The chances of dying over a 10-year period with risk on order of 10^{-3} are equivalent to annual risk changes on the order of 10^{-4}. From a sample size of 800 respondents, personal interviews were conducted in seven housing areas of Yishun (North), Redhill (South), Tampines (East), Boon Lay (West), Bukit Timah (Central), Choa Chu Kang and Sengkang.

There were three pre-survey screening criteria, (1) only respondents aged 40 to 75 were invited to participate in the survey, (2) only Singaporeans and Singapore Permanent Residents were invited to participate in the survey, (3) only respondents who understand the concept of risk reduction were invited to participate in the survey.

The questionnaire was divided into five sections. Section I begins with some demographic questions which includes respondents' personal and family health information. Section II introduces the simple concept of probability using two graphs, one shows the chance of death of 5 in 1,000 (5 coloured-grid squares out of

1,000) and another shows the chance of death of 10 in 1,000 (10 coloured-grid squares out of 1,000) over the next 10 years. The respondent was asked which of the two shows the higher risk of death. Section III presents the leading causes of death in Singapore. Section IV elicits willingness-to-pay for risk reductions of a given magnitude, occurring at a specified time, using dichotomous choice methods. Respondents were randomly assigned to one of the two sub-samples. As shown in Table 11.1, respondents in one sub-sample (wave 1) were first asked if they are willing to pay for a product that, when used and paid for over the next 10 years, will reduce baseline risk by 5 in 1,000 over the 10-year period, i.e., by 5 in 10,000 annually. In the second willingness-to-pay question, risks were reduced by 1 in 1,000, i.e., by 1 in 10,000 annually. Respondents in the second sub-sample (wave 2) were given the 1 in 1,000 risk-change question first. Section V documents respondents' characteristics such as gender, race, level of education, occupation, personal income and household income.

Early studies typically used open-ended willingness-to-pay questions, i.e., respondents were asked their maximal willingness-to-pay for a particular risk reduction. In recent years, however, closed-ended formats have become increasingly popular. In this study, the bid figures and bid structure used in the questionnaire were adapted from a contingent valuation study of Canada by Krupnick *et al.* (2002) where the figures are adjusted by the exchange rate of the two countries and inflated by average inflation rate to be expressed in 2007 Singapore dollars. All respondents were asked a set of follow-up dichotomous choice questions to

Table 11.1: Order of questions.

Group of respondents	Initial risk reduction valued	Second risk reduction valued	Future risk reduction valued
		Current risk reduction	
Wave 1	5 in 1,000	1 in 1,000	5 in 1,000
Wave 2	1 in 1,000	5 in 1,000	5 in 1,000

obtain more information about their willingness-to-pay. All willingness-to-pay dichotomous choice questions answered by "No-No" responses were followed by a question asking if the respondent is willing to pay anything at all, and if so, how much. Respondents were then asked, on a 1 to 5 scale, their degree of certainty about their responses.

From the sample size of 800 respondents, the estimated value of a statistical life in Singapore was computed by dividing the corresponding annual mean WTP figure by the size of the annual mortality risk reductions i.e., 5 in 10,000 or 1 in 10,000. The VSL is S$845,460 (US$615,950) for the 5 in 1,000 mortality risk reduction and S$2.05 million (US$1.49 million) for the 1 in 1,000 mortality risk reduction.

Cross-Country Comparison

We also documented the value of a statistical life of 13 countries. Using a proper conversion method, these estimates are reported in thousands of 2007 US dollars as shown in Table 11.2.

The above estimates suggest that Japan has the highest value of a statistical life mean of US$8.6 million followed by Switzerland of US$7.8 million and Denmark of US$3.9 million. Among these, the two newly industrialized countries, Taiwan and South Korea, have the lowest mean of US$1 million and US$646,000, respectively. The estimated value of a statistical life in Singapore between S$850,000 (US$615,950) and S$2.05 million (US$1.49 million) was close to that of South Korea and Taiwan but was lower than America's or even Australia's. However, while the figure is lower in Singapore than in other advanced economies, the sum of S$850,000 to S$2.05 million is not small when translated into public project evaluations.

Conclusion

By estimating the indigenous value of a statistical life in Singapore, it helps policymakers to refine public policy in a wide variety of areas. After the September 11 tragedy, the US government issued

Euston Quah, et al.

Table 11. 2: Number of studies with estimated mean values of a statistical life by country (in thousands of 2007 US dollars).

Country	Number of studies	Adjusted VSL	GDP per capita	GDP per capita (PPP)
		(In thousands of US$)		
Australia	1	2,216	43,312	36,258
Austria	2	3,391	45,181	38,399
Canada	5	3,667	43,485	38,435
Denmark	1	3,924	57,261	37,392
France	1	3,581	41,511	33,188
Japan	1	8,631	34,312	33,577
New Zealand	3	1,694	30,255	26,379
South Korea	2	646	19,751	24,783
Sweden	4	3,238	49,655	36,494
Switzerland	1	7,844	58,084	41,128
Taiwan	2	997	16,606	39,126
United Kingdom	7	2,378	45,575	35,134
United States	39	3,619	45,845	45,845

Note: GDP per capita and GDP per capita (PPP) are obtained from the IMF World Economic Outlook.

guidelines for compensating victims' families, dividing the payouts into economic and non-economic components. It must have been extraordinarily difficult to stick a monetary value of life in such circumstances. But the US government had to do it because the victims' families demanded some form of compensation for their loss and the public expected it. Ultimately, the question is not whether we should take on the challenge of ascribing value to life but how we should do it.

References

Alberini, A. and A. Krupnick (1998). Air Quality and Episodes of Acute Respiratory Illness in Taiwan Cities: Evidence from Survey Data. *Journal of Urban Economics*, 44, pp. 68–92.

Jones-Lee, M. W., W. Hammerton and V. Abbott (1987). The Value of Transport Safety. *Policy Journals*, UK: Newbury, Berkshire.

Krupnick, A. A. Alberini, M. Cropper, N. Simon, B. O'Brien, R. Goeree and M. Heintzelman (2002). Age, Health and Willingness to Pay for Mortality Risk Reductions: A Contingent Valuation Study of Ontario Residents. *Journal of Risk and Uncertainty*, 24, pp. 161–186.

Loehman, E. T. *et al.* (1979). Distributional Analysis of Regional Benefits and Costs of Air Quality Control. *Journal of Environmental and Management*, VI, pp. 222–243.

Quah, E. and T. L. Boon (2003). The Economic Cost of Particulate Air Pollution on Health in Singapore. *Journal of Asian Economics*, 14, pp. 73–90.

Ready, R. and S. Navrud (2006). International Benefit Transfer: Methods and Validity Tests. *Ecological Economics*, 60(2), pp. 429–434.

Viscusi, W. K. (1993). The Value of Risks to Life and Health. *Journal of Economic Literature* 31(4), pp. 1912–1946.

Viscusi, W. K. and W. N. Evans (1990). Utility Functions that Depends on Health Status: Estimates and Economic Implications. *American Economic Review* 80, pp. 353–374.

CHAPTER 12

Is the Environment a Game? Game Theoretical Analysis of the Kyoto Protocol

ERNIE G. S. TEO

G
ame theory applies mathematical analysis to strategic situations. It is used widely in modern economics to model rational behavior between agents whose decisions depend on the choices of others. In this paper, concepts of game theory will be introduced and used to analyze interactions between countries on the ratification of the Kyoto Protocol. The Kyoto Protocol is the principal update to an international environmental agreement which establishes member countries' commitment to reduce green house gas emissions. The United States is the only developed country not to have ratified the Kyoto Protocol (to reduce greenhouse gas emissions). Poor (developing) countries are also keen to shirk the responsibility of having to reduce emissions. Governments would like as many countries signing the Kyoto Protocol and committing to emission reductions except themselves. This way they can reap the benefits of reduced global warming and not have to pay for it. In game theory, this is

described as a Prisoner's Dilemma and we analyze several game theorists' take on this issue. We will discuss the incentive for countries to join a climate change agreement and why certain countries are unwilling to participate. We also examine the problem of member countries not meeting emission targets and how this free-rider problem may be addressed.

Introduction

The United Nations Framework Convention on Climate Change (UFCCC) and the Kyoto Protocol

The UFCCC is an international environment agreement (IEA) or treaty that resulted from the United Nations Conference on Environment and Development (UNCED) held in Rio de Janeiro from 3 to 14 June 1992. There are 192 UFCCC member countries that are split into three groups, Annex I countries, Annex II countries and Developing countries (see Appendix 1 for the full list). Annex I countries are industrialized countries which agreed to reduce their emission levels. Annex II countries are a subgroup of Annex I who will pay for the cost of developing countries. Developing countries are not required to reduce emissions unless Annex II countries supply the funding and technology.

The aim of the UFCCC is to stabilize greenhouse gas concentrations in the atmosphere in order to prevent harmful climate change. The treaty does not set any mandatory limits on greenhouse gas emissions but instead provides for updates or protocols which would set mandatory emission limits. The first principal update is the Kyoto Protocol which established the legally binding commitments for the reduction of greenhouse gas emissions. The Kyoto Protocol was signed on 11 December 1997 and came into effect on 16 February 2005 when Russia ratified the protocol on 18 November 2004 (this formed the majority required to bring the protocol into force). As of 2008, 183 of the UFCCC member countries have ratified the protocol. The time it took for many countries to ratify the protocol signals the difficulties and reluctance of many industrialized countries to enter into the agreement. This is because emission reductions are costly to the economy in terms of production and trade. Till today, one of the largest member countries, the United States, have not ratified the protocol. One of the reasons cited by former President George W. Bush is the exemption of China from emission reductions (which is one of the largest gross emitter of carbon dioxide). Large developed countries like China, India and Brazil have gotten out of Kyoto negotiations with no commitments on emission reductions. Developing countries put the blame on developed countries and want to continue to grow and pollute. There is a free riding problem when it comes to reducing greenhouse gas emissions (or the provision of clean air).

Game Theoretical Analysis and Environmental Cooperation

Clean air can be considered a public good,[1] and there is a problem of free-riding where clean air is enjoyed by a non-paying country. The ratification of the Kyoto Protocol can be thought of as a multiplayer version of a frequently analyzed scenario in game theory, the Prisoner's Dilemma. The Prisoner's Dilemma was first described by Merrill Flood and Melvin Dresher, two researchers at the RAND Corporation in 1950, as a game of cooperation and conflict. Two prisoners are kept in separate jail cells. They can either keep quiet and "Cooperate" with each other or "Defect" by giving evidence against each other. They choose either "Cooperate" or "Defect" without knowing what the other person will do — this is known as a simultaneous game in game theory. If both prisoners keeps quiet ("Cooperate"), they will both go to jail for a year. If both choose to "Defect", they each go to jail for 5 years. If one choose "Cooperate" but the other choose "Defect"

---

[1] A good is known as a public good when it is non-excludable (you cannot exclude non-payers from consuming it) and non-rival (one person's consumption has no effect on the amount available to others).

then the defector goes free and the other prisoner goes to jail for 10 years. Although it makes sense to "Cooperate", choosing "Defect" gives you a better payoff no matter what your opponent does. The following table summarizes the game in what is called a payoff matrix:

Table 12.1:   Prisoner's Dilemma game.

Prisoner A		Prisoner B	
		Cooperate	Defect
	Cooperate	−1,−1	−10,0
	Defect	0,−10	−5,−5

No matter what Prisoner B does, Prisoner A is always better off choosing "Defect", this is known as a dominant strategy. Prisoner B also has a dominant strategy of choosing "Defect". If both players play rationally, they each get 5 years which is worse than a cooperative outcome of 1 year each. This non-cooperative outcome is also known as a Nash equilibrium[2] (named after Nobel Prize winner John Nash).

The Prisoner's Dilemma game can be applied to many real life situations such as two companies deciding on a price war. The negotiations over greenhouse gas emissions can also be applied to a classic Prisoner's Dilemma. If all countries reduce emissions and one does not, the non-participating country "free rides" on the efforts of the other countries. The free-rider gets all the benefits of cleaner air without the costs involved in reducing its own emissions. If there are no countries reducing emissions, then it also makes no sense to reduce emissions, as one country's effort is not substantial. Therefore, it may be inevitable that countries may choose to "Defect" and not take any action.

---

[2] Nash equilibrium refers to a equilibrium of strategies where no player can gain by changing his own strategy, assuming that other players' strategies remain constant.

Using the idea of the Prisoner's Dilemma, we examine a country's benefit derived from its emissions. Following Finus (2002), we assume that welfare of country i (π_i) is given as follows:

$$\pi_i = \beta_i(e_i) - \varphi_i \left(\sum_{j=1}^{N} e_j \right) \tag{1}$$

e_i represents country i's emissions and $\beta_i(e_i)$ is the benefits generated by country i's emissions in terms of production of goods.

$$\varphi_i \left(\sum_{j=1}^{N} e_j \right)$$

is the damage caused to country i by global emissions, N is the total number of countries. If a country does not care about environmental damage, it will continue to produce until the marginal benefit of emissions is zero. We call this emission level e_i^{max}, the largest possible level of emissions (no abatement).

If there were no cooperation between countries, each country will maximize its own welfare. Each country will thus equate its marginal benefit to marginal costs of emissions,

$$\beta_i'(e_i) = \varphi_i' \left(\sum_{j=1}^{N} e_j \right) \tag{2}$$

The emission level which solves this equation is e_i^N. The set of emission levels chosen by all countries is given by

$$e^N = (e_1^N, \ldots, e_N^N),$$

this is the non-cooperative or Nash equilibrium.[3] We can assume that this is the level of emissions before the Kyoto protocol. This level of emissions is lower than e_i^{max}. Governments would choose

---

[3] This corresponds to the (Defect, Defect) outcome in the Prisoner's Dilemma.

to reduce some emissions if they are aware of the damage emissions are doing to their environment.

If a country is fully cooperative, then the government should consider the damage caused in other countries as well.[4] The welfare function would become:

$$\pi_i = \beta_i(e_i) - \sum_{j=1}^{N} \varphi_i \left(\sum_{j=1}^{N} e_j \right) \qquad (3)$$

The optimal solution to this welfare function would require that marginal benefit equals the total marginal damages in all countries. This fully cooperative solution would also be the social optimum. Marginal benefits would be equal across countries. This solution would generate the highest global welfare and will result in lower emissions than the Nash equilibrium.

Although the social optimum is the most efficient, many countries would be reluctant to cut emissions by a large amount as this will affect their competitiveness. Emissions between the social optimum and the Nash equilibrium would be an intermediate solution and involves internalizing some global externalities. One such solution is the "uniform proportional emission reduction" method where emissions are reduced by a certain percentage compared to the status quo. This is similar to the Kyoto Protocol where emission reduction targets are based on the emissions of 38 countries in 1990. This solution is inefficient as the marginal benefits are not equalized across countries. Nevertheless, it can achieve a higher global welfare than the Nash equilibrium.

There is an incentive for governments to coordinate on emissions rather than just act alone. Despite this, countries are having difficulties coming to an agreement with the Kyoto Protocol. There are difficulties with coordinating membership and terms because 1) membership is voluntary, 2) all parties must agree on the terms and 3) the agreement has to be enforced by the parties themselves. The non-compulsory nature of the Kyoto Protocol leads to

---

[4] This corresponds to the (Cooperate, Cooperate) outcome in the Prisoner's Dilemma.

free-rider problems. There are two types of free-rider problems with a treaty on greenhouse gas reductions. The first type are countries who do not sign the agreement or countries with low or no abatement burdens. To solve this we need to think about the incentives for a country to sign the agreement. We will examine this type of problem in Section 2. The second type of free-riders are countries that sign the agreement but do not meet the targets. We need credible punishment strategies for the sustainability of the treaty. Section 3 will deals with stability and enforcement issues.

The Participation Problem

One major problem with the UFCCC is that many countries are not willing to ratify the protocol. Governments maximizing their own country's welfare will find it beneficial to free ride instead of committing to reducing emissions. Future protocols to the UFCCC would also require ratification and this would lead to the same problem again.[5] To analyze this problem we can look at a game theory framework called the Reduced Form Game.

The Reduced Form Game

The Reduced Form game represents a multiple staged game by reducing it to one stage. This is done with backward induction; we first consider what would happen in the last stage and work backwards to the first. There are three stages to the creation of a emissions reduction agreement; the countries first decide if they will join the coalition, in the next stage the level of emissions are decided. In the third stage, the welfare gains from reduced emission are distributed. If countries are asymmetric, some countries may get a net loss and this can be balanced with transfers from countries with a net gain. Therefore, a country would join the coalition if its welfare at the end of the third stage (if it joins) is larger than if it did not join.

---

[5] The treaty to replace the Kyoto Protocol is expected to be adopted at the UNCCC at Copenhagen in December 2009.

When countries are heterogeneous (have different welfare functions), then not all countries will join the coalition. A coalition is considered stable if no country wants to join or leave it, that is where no country's welfare will be better off if it changes its position (coalition member to non-member or vice versa). Internal stability is when a member country does not want to leave the coalition; this can be summarized with the following:

$$\pi_i^J(N^*,e^*) - \pi_i^{NJ}(N^*-1,e^{*\prime}) \geq 0. \qquad (4)$$

The welfare from remaining in the coalition must be greater than welfare if the country leaves the coalition. $e^{*\prime}$ refers to the re-optimized emission strategies given the change in the number of member countries. A coalition is externally stable when non-members do not want to join the coalition, or:

$$\pi_i^J(N^*+1,e^{*\prime}) - \pi_i^{NJ}(N^*,e^*) \leq 0. \qquad (5)$$

The welfare from joining the coalition is smaller than the welfare of the country if it remains a non-member. When countries' welfare functions are different or heterogeneous, a stable coalition will not contain all countries. This is because some countries may get lower welfare as a result of reduced emissions. For all countries to join the coalition, it may be necessary to implement a more symmetric welfare distribution system rather than the most efficient one. The "uniform proportional emission reduction" method is one such system. Another way is to use a compensation system where countries with net welfare gains transfer the benefits to countries with net welfare losses. If countries receive the same net benefit (they are homogeneous) then no transfers are necessary in the third stage.

Discussion

When many countries are involved in the externality problem and the costs of reducing emissions is small compared to the amount of environmental damages, then global cooperation is the best outcome. Academic studies have found that any coalition, whatever the size, will increase individual and global welfare and reduce global pollution (Finus, 2002).

A coalition will have better success at reducing global pollution if it considers leakage effects from non-member countries and it would be better to observe the reactions of non-members first before choosing a reduction strategy.

A small coalition may be able to achieve more than a large group as there is less conflict of interests within the group. The results in Bauer (1992) show that countries with similar interests will form a coalition and act as one country. These small coalitions can then join to form a larger coalition. It may not be realistic to assume that several countries can act as one entity, but this result indicates that smaller countries with similar interests can first form a coalition and then sequentially expand (including countries with similar interests as the group as a whole) and form a larger coalition.

As pointed out in Carraro (1998), an agreement signed by all countries is likely to be unsuccessful if it only includes emission targets. Even if transfers are included, a global coalition may not be formed due to commitment problems (agreeing to reduce emissions may not be credible if the country is better off by not meeting the targets; we will examine this problem in the next section). The equilibrium coalition structure found in Carraro (1998) is characterized by several coalitions. This implies that the likely outcome may be regional agreements on climate change rather than a global one.

The Stability and Enforcement Problem

This section deals with the second type of free-rider problem — member countries who do not meet their target. We know that there is a Prisoner's Dilemma problem with greenhouse gas emission reductions; one way to solve the Prisoner's Dilemma is through repeated interactions. In the following sections we will use the Infinite Repeated games framework to outline possible solutions or strategies which can be undertaken to ensure that countries stick to their targets.

Infinite Repeated Games

In an Infinite Repeated Prisoner's Dilemma game, the game is played repeatedly to perpetuity. A more realistic assumption is that the end of the game is not known with certainty; each player chooses his current period's strategy without knowing for certain if the game ends in the next period. The UFCCC can be described as an infinite game; even though protocols may replace each other, there is no specified end date to the Convention.

With the right punishment strategy and repeated interactions, the (Cooperate, Cooperate) outcome in the Prisoner's Dilemma game can be an equilibrium. A stable strategy in an Infinite Repeated game is one where the punishment for deviation is sufficient to prevent free-riding, that is no country deviates and no punishments are carried out. One such strategy is what we call a trigger strategy; this is a dynamic strategy as it is a collection of instructions on what to do at each point of time for each situation which may arise. The trigger strategy stipulates that the contract be suspended once deviation is detected. That is once one country cheats, all the other countries revert to the status quo emission levels. For this strategy to work, the required condition is as follows:

$$\pi_i^*(e^*) \geq (1-\delta_i)\pi_i^F(e_i^F, e_{-i}^*) + \delta_i\pi_i^N(e^N) \tag{6}$$

The average welfare from complying must be greater than the average welfare from free-riding and subsequently, being punished. δ is a discount factor which is given by $p_i/(1+r_i)$ where p_i is country i's estimated probability that the game will continue and r_i is the discount rate. Equation (6) can be rearranged as follows:

$$\delta_i \geq \frac{\pi_i^F - \pi_i^*}{\pi_i^F - \pi_i^N} = \delta_i^{\min} \tag{7}$$

When the actual δ is greater than δ_i^{min}, cooperation can be sustained and country i will not cheat on emission reduction targets. In fact, it can be shown that a punishment strategy which punishes for a certain number of periods is enough to sustain cooperation. A punishment strategy will work as long as the discounted stream of welfare from complying is greater than the welfare that can be obtained from free-riding in one period and being punished for a certain number of periods. All member countries cooperating can be a stable equilibrium.

There can be a number of possible strategies which can be used to sustain cooperation. Axelrod (1984) found that when the Prisoner's Dilemma is played repeatedly, cooperative behavior eventually emerges. In the late 1970s, Robert Axelrod invited social scientists to submit strategies which were pitted against others in the Repeated Prisoner's Dilemma game using computer simulations. The winning strategy (highest payoffs after a certain number of rounds) was what is known as the Tit-for-Tat strategy. The Tit-for-Tat strategy starts off with cooperation and then mirrors the opponent's last move. If your opponent cheated in the last period, you will cheat in the current period. The essence of the Tit-for-Tat strategy boils down to four simple rules as described by Axelrod (1984) and reiterated by Liebretch (2007) for the emissions reduction game. The four rules are:

- **Be Nice** — Cooperate in the beginning and do not be the first to cheat. Countries should sign any agreement which is economically viable.
- **Be Retaliatory** — If your opponent cheats, you must punish in the next period. Find ways to hurt countries (trade sanctions, etc.) that have not taken action and make it clear that it is in response to their actions on climate change.
- **Be Forgiving** — If your opponent changes his ways, you have to restore cooperation in the next period. When countries that refused to sign previously decides to join, member countries should welcome them and provide necessary assistance. Signal that cooperative behavior will be rewarded.

- **Be Clear** — Be consistent, make it clear you are following the above three strategies. If your opponent knows that, then it will be to his advantage to cooperate. Let all countries know exactly how you will behave.

Therefore, if the four rules can be adhered to by all countries and the Tit-for-Tat strategy is used, cooperation among member countries can be sustained. There will be no incentives to fall short on the emissions target and overall increase in welfare will be high.

Discussion

Liebretch (2007) uses the four rules of Tit-for-Tat and evaluates the major players of the Kyoto Protocol and their strategies. Below is a summary of this analysis:

Europe

Europe is being nice, by signing and agreeing to cut emissions by 20 percent. However, it is not being retaliatory; Europe has a reputation of being unwilling to retaliate. For example, it did not apply any sanctions against Greece when it was found that they falsified data when it applied to join the European Union. On the forgiveness front, Europe has already signaled that it will increase its reduction targets if other nations like China and India climbs on board. Europe has also always been clear on its stance in climate change negotiations. Therefore, Europe needs to become retaliatory in order for the Tit-for-Tat strategy to work. They need to find ways where they can punish countries that are refusing to sign or not meeting targets. Some suggestions include naming and shaming, carbon-related import taxes or more general exclusions from the benefits of trade.

US

The US, on the other hand, are not being nice; they start off negotiations by defecting. The US's strong points are being retaliatory and forgiving. They have not only shown on numerous occasions that they are very willing to retaliate against opponents, they are also forgiving towards their former opponents such as the help rendered to the former Soviet Union following the fall of communism. The Asia-Pacific Partnership on Clean Development and Climate Change involves transfers of technology from the US and can be seen as a reward to developing countries for cooperating on climate change. The US can be unclear as its political system has many conflicting interests and is not transparent to outsiders. The US should start taking meaningful action and pass some bills which will take aggressive measures on emission reductions.

Developing World

China, India and Brazil have escaped Kyoto negotiations with no limits on their allowed emissions. This may seem like a good result for them but it signals a refusal to cooperate (or to be nice). They also showed a lack of forgiveness by making industrialized nations pay for their previous emissions. The developing world should commit to sharing global efforts by emphasizing "common" rather than "differentiated" responsibilities. If not, developing countries may find themselves on the receiving end of non-cooperation from other countries.

Conclusion

Using two basic game theoretical frameworks, we analyzed the problems of membership and enforcement of the Kyoto Protocol. From the Reduced Form Game framework we found that similar countries have more incentive to form agreements. Therefore, smaller coalitions (or regional agreements) may be a starting point leading to larger global cooperation on climate change. The Kyoto protocol sets emission targets for 38 industrial countries (the EU is considered one entity). Of the 38 countries, only the United States has not ratified the protocol. Game theoretical analysis shows that although this group of 38 countries is small, it will have an impact on reducing carbon emissions. The leakage effect from countries with no emission targets like China may become large in the future. Therefore, it makes sense that some developing countries be included in future protocols. Since the protocol is not enforceable (countries who cannot meet targets can always choose not to ratify it), the terms needed for countries to participate have to make them better off. For developing countries to sign up, transfer payments would be needed to compensate for loss in emission benefits. This may be hard to enforce in real life. The Infinite Repeated Game framework demonstrated how to enforce a cooperative agreement. A good punishment strategy will ensure that no member country free rides. This can be achieved by following the Tit-for-Tat strategy and ensuring that the four rules are followed by all member countries. Further analysis by economic scholars discusses many interesting results. For example, Chander *et al.* (1999) show that an appropriate emissions quota and trading scheme can be equivalent to the global optimum.

In the game theoretical analysis discussed, we assume that governments care only to maximize their own countries' welfare. This means that they will act opportunistically and take a free ride whenever it benefits them. This may not be realistic as reputation may have an effect on governments' decisions. Governments care about what their actions will do to voters' opinion of them; therefore if there is strong public support for emission reductions, this will somewhat affect their decisions. Governments may also care about its reputation towards other governments as they need to consider future interactions such as trade agreements. Therefore, much more complex analysis is needed to thoroughly analyze the situation with the Kyoto Protocol. Although some restrictive assumptions were made in our analysis, it gives us many interesting insights to the cooperative problem of the Kyoto Protocol. This can give policy makers some direction where future negotiations will lead and also provides insights as to how cooperation among countries can be attained.

Appendix 1 — UFCCC Member Countries

Afghanistan, Albania, Algeria, Angola, Antigua and Barbuda, Argentina, Armenia, Australia$^{\#\wedge}$, Austria$^{\#\wedge}$, Azerbaijan, Bahamas, Bahrain, Bangladesh, Barbados, Belarus$^{\#}$, Belgium$^{\#\wedge}$, Belize, Benin, Bhutan, Bolivia, Bosnia and Herzegovina, Botswana, Brazil, Brunei, Bulgaria$^{\#}$, Burkina Faso, Myanmar, Burundi, Cambodia, Cameroon, Canada$^{\#\wedge}$, Cape Verde, Central African Republic, Chad, Chile, China, Colombia, Comoros, Democratic Republic of the Congo, Republic of the Congo, Cook Islands, Costa Rica, Côte d'Ivoire, Croatia$^{\#}$, Cuba, Cyprus, Czech Republic$^{\#}$, Denmark$^{\#\wedge}$, Djibouti, Dominica, Dominican Republic, Ecuador, Egypt, El Salvador, Equatorial Guinea, Eritrea, Estonia$^{\#}$, Ethiopia, European Union, Fiji, Finland$^{\#\wedge}$, France$^{\#\wedge}$, Gabon, Gambia, Georgia, Germany$^{\#\wedge}$, Ghana, Greece$^{\#\wedge}$, Grenada, Guatemala, Guinea, Guinea–Bissau, Guyana, Haiti, Honduras, Hungary$^{\#}$, Iceland$^{\#\wedge}$, India, Indonesia, Iran, Ireland$^{\#\wedge}$, Israel, Italy$^{\#\wedge}$, Jamaica, Japan$^{\#\wedge}$, Jordan, Kazakhstan, Kenya, Kiribati, North Korea, South Korea, Kuwait, Kyrgyzstan, Laos, Latvia$^{\#}$, Lebanon, Lesotho, Liberia, Libya, Liechtenstein$^{\#}$, Lithuania$^{\#}$, Luxembourg$^{\#\wedge}$, Republic of Macedonia, Madagascar, Malawi, Malaysia, Maldives, Mali, Malta, Marshall Islands, Mauritania, Mauritius, Mexico, Federated States of Micronesia, Moldova, Monaco$^{\#}$, Mongolia, Montenegro, Morocco, Mozambique, Namibia, Nauru, Nepal, Netherlands$^{\#\wedge}$, New Zealand$^{\#\wedge}$, Nicaragua, Niger, Nigeria, Niue, Norway$^{\#\wedge}$, Oman, Pakistan, Palau, Panama, Papua New Guinea, Paraguay, Peru, Philippines, Poland$^{\#}$, Portugal$^{\#\wedge}$, Qatar, Romania$^{\#}$, Russia$^{\#}$, Rwanda, Saint Kitts and Nevis, Saint Lucia, Saint Vincent and the Grenadines, Samoa, San Marino, Sao Tome and Principe, Saudi Arabia, Senegal, Serbia, Seychelles, Sierra Leone, Singapore, Slovakia$^{\#}$, Slovenia$^{\#}$, Solomon Islands, South Africa, Spain$^{\#\wedge}$, Sri Lanka, Sudan, Suriname, Swaziland, Sweden$^{\#\wedge}$, Switzerland$^{\#\wedge}$, Syria, Tajikistan, Tanzania, Thailand, Timor-Leste. Togo, Tonga, Trinidad and Tobago, Tunisia, Turkey$^{\#}$, Turkmenistan, Tuvalu, Uganda, Ukraine$^{\#}$, United Arab Emirates, United Kingdom$^{\#\wedge}$, United States$^{\#\wedge}$, Uruguay, Uzbekistan, Vanuatu, Venezuela, Vietnam, Yemen, Zambia and Zimbabwe.

Annex I country

^ Annex II country

References

Axelrod, R. M. (1984). *The Evolution of Cooperation*. Basic Books.
Bauer, A. (1992). International Cooperation over Greenhouse Gas Abatement. Munich, Germany: Mimeo of the Seminar für emporosche Wirtschaftsforchung, University of Munich.
Carraro, C. (1998). Beyond Kyoto. A Game — Theoretic Perspective. OECD workshop on Climate Change and Economic Modelling. Background Analysis for the Kyoto Protocol, Paris, 1998.
Chander, P., H. Tulkens, J. Ypersele and S. Willems (1999). The Kyoto Protocol: An Economic and Game Theoretical Interpretation. Economic Theory for the Environment. Essays in Honour of Karl-GÄoran MÄaler.
Finus, M. (2002). Game Theory and International Environmental Cooperation: Any Practical Application? In *Controlling Global Warming*. Edward Elgar Publishing, pp. 9–104.
Liebreich, M. (2007). *How to Save the Planet: Be Nice, Retaliatory, Forgiving & Clear*. New Energy Finance Ltd, 2007.

Index